SEASONS *of* WIRRAL

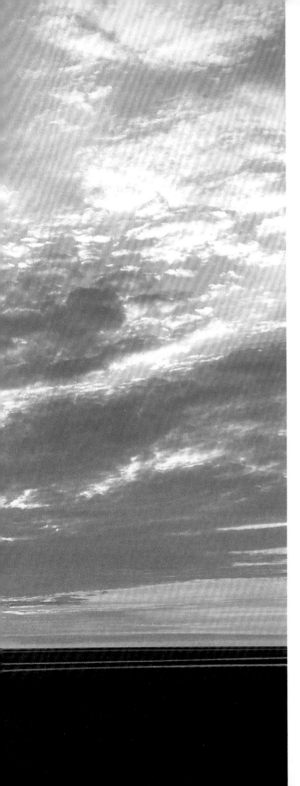

SEASONS *of* WIRRAL

Wirral's wildlife and landscape through the year

Guy Huntington *&* Kenneth Burnley

THE SILVER BIRCH PRESS
WIRRAL • CHESHIRE

First published in Great Britain in 1994 by
The Silver Birch Press, 248 Telegraph Road, Heswall, Wirral L60 7SG

Photographs copyright © Guy Huntington 1994
Text copyright © Kenneth J. Burnley 1994

ISBN 0 9517961 1 9

Design, layout & typesetting by Kenneth Burnley at Irby, Wirral
Origination by Primary Four Limited, Moreton, Wirral
Printed by Printfine Limited, Liverpool

Dedication

We dedicate this book to all who help to protect, conserve and preserve the wild, beautiful and natural places of Wirral.

Also by Kenneth Burnley and Guy Huntington:

Images of Wirral – a celebration in words and photographs

Contents

Title-page photograph: Sunset over the Dee Estuary and Hilbre

Endpapers: A pair of Canada geese, backlit by morning sunlight, fly over dew-drenched fields, Montgomery Hill, near West Kirby

Foreword

THE Wirral Peninsula is a unique and fascinating place: within this small tongue of land, just eighteen miles by eight, bounded on the north by the Irish Sea, on the east by the River Mersey, and on the west by the River Dee, there is a wealth of natural interest that belies its size. The richness and diversity of its landscape and natural habitats, with their animals, birds and plants, is one of the most attractive and, to the newcomer and stranger, most surprising aspects of the place.

Because of this richness and diversity, Wirral has often been called a 'microcosm of England', for almost every aspect of the English landscape can be found here: wood, river, heathland, valley, coast, estuary, suburb, town, countryside. We have, sadly, no mountains: but we do have the glorious panorama of the Welsh Hills which can be seen from many parts of the peninsula!

The authors of this book have come to know and love this richness that is Wirral over many years. We have spent countless hours walking its woods and field-paths, wading its coastal waters, watching its wildlife at close range. The fruits of those efforts – labour is the wrong word, for this has been a joyous experience – are recorded in these pages, in words and photographs. We invite both resident and visitor alike to share some of those experiences with us, through these beautiful and, in some ways, unique images.

Some of the places described and shown here you will recognise; some may perhaps be new to you. We have attempted to portray these lovely places as we see them during the course of the four seasons. There is, of course, no such thing as a typical year in these parts; but we believe that this book presents the peninsula and its natural places in a very special way.

Most of the places shown in this book are accessible to the public, and owned and managed by the local authority, the National Trust, or Cheshire Wildlife Trust.

9

As such they are fully protected from development. However, the fragility of some of these places is very evident: that is often part of their beauty. If this book helps raise an awareness of the richness and beauty of Wirral's natural places, so that these places will be afforded greater protection in the future, the effort will have been worth while.

Guy Huntington and Kenneth Burnley
August 1994

Right: Sea-water run-off between the islands, Hilbre

10

Introduction

WE are all influenced by the seasons – who would not own up to the thrill of seeing the first snowdrops or celandines in the early months of the year; the creamy blanket of may-blossom along our hedgerows in early summer; the splash of colour from wildflowers in the coastal dunes later in the summer; the rich, fiery pageant of autumnal glory in woods and hedgerows; and the cold, clear crispness of our rural landscapes in the depths of winter?

Although most of us today live and work away from the fields, without that intimate contact with the living, changing world that our ancestors knew, there is still, deep down within our beings, a strong sensitivity to the annual cycle. It influences our lives in so many ways, despite twentieth-century comforts – our cars and our centrally-heated homes – which insulate us from close contact with so many aspects of the changing seasons.

Perhaps we who live in Wirral are more fortunate than many in this respect, for the unfolding of the seasons is very evident in the peninsula's rich variety of habitats: from the diversity of our urban and suburban gardens, to the high, rugged, heathy moors; from the woods and copses to the seashores of the northern coast; from the pastoral landscapes of rural Wirral to the bird-life of the estuaries.

Sadly, the beauty of the seasons is fleeting: none of nature's gifts last for more than a few short weeks. The daffodils of April wither and fade rapidly in the warming sunshine of May; the migrant birds massing over the estuaries forsake our shores for more northern climes in spring, and depart for the south in autumn; summer hedgerow blossoms turn to reddening berries within weeks of flowering; autumnal colours are soon shaken from the trees by equinoctial storms, and the ripening fruits are eagerly devoured by man, bird and beast; and the rare snowfalls that bedeck twigs and branches melt in the warmth of the daytime sun.

Sometimes the magic of our seasons' images is so delectable that we wish to garner the scenes, to preserve them, to capture their beauty for ever. Often, in the cold and drabness of a winter's day, I long for the soft beauty and fragrance of a wild rose, or honeysuckle, as they bloom on mellow June evenings in the hedgerows around Irby Hill. And on those rare, sweltering days of high summer, when the land is yellow and parched, I remember the sweet softness of autumnal rainfall, caressing the earth and enshrouding our heaths, woods and fields with a veil of cool mist.

But we too often fail to enjoy the seasons for what they are, for both the large-scale beauties of our landscapes, and the smaller, but no less beautiful images. Richard Jefferies reminds us of our failings when he writes:

'Only by walking hand in hand with nature, only by a reverent and loving study of the mysteries for ever around us, is it possible to disabuse the mind of the narrow view, the contracted belief that time is now and eternity tomorrow. Eternity is today. The goldfinches and the tiny caterpillars, the brilliant sun, if looked at lovingly and thoughtfully, will lift the soul out of the smaller life of human care that is of selfish aims, bounded by seventy years, into the greater, the limitless life which has been going on over universal space from endless ages past, which is going on now, and which will for ever and ever, in one form or another, continue to proceed.'

Jefferies was right to emphasise the continuity of nature, of life. For although we portray the seasons in this book as a course of events with a beginning and an end, in nature's year there is no last page, no final endpaper: in nature the cycle begins all over again, as if we had read through the book once, and immediately pick it up and turn again to the first page.

The seasons in Wirral, then, are timeless, without beginning or end. They are a perpetual cycle of beauty, of wonder, of interest to those who go out to see, to smell, and to listen. Although captured here in picture-form and in word-form, these images cannot convey completely the full wonder, the beautiful reality of clear spring morns on the sands of Dee, of tender summer evenings in Dibbinsdale, of autumn mists on Thurstaston Hill, or winter snows across mid-Wirral fields. What the images contained in this book *will* do, though, is convey the richness and variety of our natural heritage; and take the reader, at any time of the year, to those lovely places that make up so much of the Wirral Peninsula.

Right: Wall Brown butterfly

Spring

Hawthorn blossoms at
Wirral Country Park Visitors' Centre

SPRING. Did any word ever quicken the heart, raise the spirit, gladden the mind, as much as this? In this short word is captured the essence of life itself: hope, optimism, new birth. In the darkest depths of the worst of winters, when the nights are still long, the mornings dark, and dankness fills the air and permeates our hearts, the thought of spring – with its sure promise of light, colour and warmth – lifts the aching spirit, strengthens winter-weary bodies, and offers something for each of us to live for.

It is surely not possible for anyone who has even an ounce of love for our natural surroundings to fail to notice the subtle but sure changes which take place early in the year. A few weeks after the winter solstice, we notice the slight lengthening of the daylight hours; we see the sun setting each day a little further to the northern sector of the sky. Although the weather and the outside temperatures may not show it, nature is starting to respond, ever so slowly, to the lengthening days.

We see the first changes perhaps in

sheltered woodlands – in Dibbinsdale, or Arrowe – where, hidden beneath last year's dead grasses, a few primrose buds poke forth on short stalks, to burst into flower on mild February days. In the same glades, the year's first snowdrops and celandines light up the otherwise gloomy ground and, despite hard frosts still to come, a couple of early marsh-marigolds show signs of life.

Except in very hard winters, which we rarely experience here in Wirral, our favourite and much-loved songbirds are quick to tell us that new beginnings are afoot. How lovely to hear the short but nonetheless beautiful song of thrush and blackbird in late January; one of my lasting memories is of listening to the pure notes of a thrush, singing his heart out from the tall trees near Caldy crossroads as I walked home late one very mild New Year's evening!

Some springs are long, gentle, drawn-out affairs, starting early in a mild winter, the flow interrupted by brief spells of cold, sharp weather, with nature's pageant spreading itself over the months from January to May. Such springs are typical of

Left: Sedge warbler

Right: Rhododendrons by the Mere, Royden Park, Frankby

these parts: pleasant, but not memorable.

Occasionally, though, we experience a 'Sudden Spring'. To enjoy these we have usually endured a long, hard winter: stubborn anticyclonic weather systems bringing in bitterly cold easterly winds from the continent, with their attendant frosts and snows. By March, we wonder if spring will ever show even the smallest spark of life: but then, suddenly, the wind turns back to the sweet west; temperatures rise by ten degrees, the ground starts to thaw; a soft, gentle, warm rain falls and, almost overnight, nature springs to life, making up for weeks of lost time.

In such springs we see the usual pageant compressed and, instead of a long succession of blooming, blossoming, growing, greening, it all happens at once: our senses are overwhelmed by the beauty, the sheer power, of nature coming from death to exquisite life.

Where are my favourite spring places?

Perhaps the woodlands of Wirral. Can there be a more joyous spring experience than early-morning May walks through the majestic woods of Arrowe, Eastham, or Dibbinsdale, with low sunlight shining through fresh, gossamer-green beech foliage, a myriad of songbirds sending their pure notes to the high, green vaults above?

Perhaps the joy of seeing favourite

flowers – rare primroses, cowslips, or early orchids – springing up once more in old haunts. Or the reappearance of migrant birds around the Wirral coast, after their long journey northwards from tropical winter homes.

All of these, and many more, make springtime in Wirral such an exciting experience – an experience to be enjoyed, treasured; for the events of the season are fleeting, and the heaviness of high summer soon makes the freshness and beauty of spring just a fleeting memory . . .

Left: Early snowdrops carpet the banks of the Clatter Brook, near Raby Mere

Right: A family of Canada geese on the pond at Gilroy Nature Park, West Kirby. This pair had raised a larger brood than usual; generally only five to six eggs are laid

The Clatter Brook, Thornton Wood

The golden-yellow carpets of lesser celandine bursting into flower in early spring are the surest reminders that winter's worst is behind us. Formerly bare patches of earth by verges and hedgebanks come to life seemingly overnight as the air and soil warm up; and bright, sunny days bring these lovely, star-like flowers into full bloom.

It's not easy to select the best places to see this widespread plant, for it grows everywhere, but it does look its best on the lane-banks around Gayton and Storeton; and alongside the swiftly-flowing brooks of Dibbinsdale, where it mingles with other springtime plants – moschatel and forget-me-not – to form a rich flower-bed which any gardener would envy!

The plant has been widely used in herbal remedies for various diseases, and the petals were gathered for use as a bright yellow dye.

Kingcups in Foxes Wood, Raby

The rather colourless early spring days in our Wirral woodlands are enlivened by the bright yellow patches of kingcups, or marsh marigold, with their large buttercup-type flowers and shiny leaves. Boggy sections of the woods at Dibbinsdale and Arrowe, and small copses up and down the peninsula are the places to find these lovely plants, which in olden days were often hung over the cattle byres on May Day to protect the livestock from evil spirits.

Waterfall,
Foxes Wood, Dibbinsdale

The abundant showers of early spring
ensure a constant supply of running water
in Wirral's brooks and streams, and the
ancient river-valleys of Dibbinsdale echo
to the splash and trickle of water cascading
over rocks and stones.

The small but constant force of
running water over aeons of time has
etched and carved deep clefts into the very
fabric of Wirral's land-surface, forming
wild, rugged valleys which, because of their
unsuitability for man's use, are rich in
vegetation and sanctuaries for wildlife of
all kinds.

Their rich springtime flora of dogs
mercury, wood sorrel and wood anemone
point to a long, continuous period of
growth and development; and a fine cover
of native trees – oak, ash, and hazel –
clothe the valley-sides.

Beside the streams grow clumps of
primroses, celandine and violets; mosses,
lichens and liverworts clothe the damp,
water-washed rock faces; and, in this, the
springtime of the year, the woods become
a cathedral of bird-song from dawn to
dusk, a beautiful chorus celebrating the
rebirth of the year.

Eastham woods: 'from knolls here and there you get bright glimpses of the river, and as you tread the white and gold of daisy and celandine, you see the primrose stars beginning to shine from green crepe leaves amongst the withered wood-drift of last year . . .'

Today, one has to search carefully for this elusive plant, but it still grows in quiet, unknown corners of Arrowe, Shotwick, Dibbinsdale; and in other secret places around Wirral. Its unexpected discovery on a lovely April day is one of the delights of spring.

Primroses, Intake Wood, Dibbinsdale

The freshness of early spring is captured in the delicate flowers and subtle scent of the primrose, a plant which, probably more than any other, typifies for most people the precious but fleeting character of the season.

I have seen Wirral primroses in flower in the early days of the new year, in a particularly mild winter; but typically the yellow flower-heads bloom in March and April.

Primroses were used in olden times to cure rheumatism and gout, and an infusion of the roots was said to cure headaches. Love potions were prepared from the flower-petals.

Gone, alas, are the days, not so long ago, when a Wirral rambler could write of

Stanney Wood, near Ellesmere Port

The lengthening days and rising temperatures are bringing forth the greening of Wirral's woods and hedgerows, as buds and blossoms burst into life.

In the woods, the plants and shrubs of the woodland floor are the first to respond to the season, taking advantage of the daylight unobstructed by the taller canopy of the mature trees which will put the undergrowth into deep shade as the year advances.

Already, the ferns are unfolding and honeysuckle is breaking into leaf, and a faint film of gossamer green clothes the silver birches as they start to break bud.

Great spotted woodpecker, Caldy Hill

One of the strangest sounds in our woods is the echoing drumming of this woodpecker against a dead bough. Often heard, but rarely seen, this lovely bird is widespread throughout Wirral's woodlands where, at this time of the year, pairs are coming together to nest and breed.

Stanney Wood,
near Ellesmere Port

At this time of the year, many flowers carpet our woodland floors, taking advantage of the higher light levels for their short growing season. Large clumps of stitchwort carpet the pathsides in Stanney Wood: an unusual place in which to find this plant, which usually prefers hedgebanks and field-edges, where it straggles amongst the long grasses for support.

If you pick this plant, you will notice that the stems are brittle and break easily; indeed, this was associated with supposed healing properties for mending broken bones in bygone times, hence its botanical name which means 'whole' and 'bone'.

Its common name, however, refers to its use as a cure for stitches and similar abdominal pains, when it was mixed with acorns and supped in wine as a standard remedy. It was also regarded as a 'thunder flower', the picking of which was supposed to bring on thunderstorms.

Seeing stitchwort in Stanney Woods reminds me of the variety to be found amongst Wirral's woodlands. Each wood is unique in its age, its aspect, its atmosphere. No two are alike. The woods of Dibbinsdale are wild, ragged, ancient:

those of Arrowe are park-like, formal, but no less beautiful. The pine woods of Royden Park have a flavour, a smell, of their own: no flowers grow beneath that dark, shady canopy. They are gloomy, mysterious, without seasons. The birch-woods of Caldy Hill are light, bright, airy, full of seasonal character and lit by the reflected light of the estuary. I think too of the west-facing woods on Burton Hill, the bracken man-high; and then the rugged, stony, ivy-covered slopes of Storeton Woods, hiding secrets of man's early works in the area.

I look at the wind-blown trees clothing the Dungeon Woods on high lands overlooking the Dee, and the lofty, majestic oaks and beeches at sheltered Eastham, looking out over an equally majestic river.

I do not believe that the Wirral peninsula was ever well wooded: too much of our land is shallow-soiled, rocky, and battered by salt-laden, maritime winds. The Wirral Forest was not a wooded forest, but a hunting-ground. Then I remember the peat-beds of Meols, the decayed tree-stumps and leaf-mould of six thousand years ago: and I cannot make up my mind.

But it matters not: this season shows our woodlands at their best: full of life, light, and new birth.

Thornton Wood, near Dibbinsdale

The late spring sunshine has brought into flower the glorious bluebells which carpet the floors of many of Wirral's woods. Their dark, shiny-green leaves have been pushing slowly up through the decaying leaf-litter since the dark days of mid-winter, but they have needed the warm kiss of May sunlight to bring to fruition this last, prolific display of woodland colour before the heavy midsummer canopy brings sterile gloom to these wild woods of mid-Wirral.

The bluebells love our west-coast climate, with its mild, moisture-laden breezes; they flourish in many of Wirral's woods and sheltered copses, from the Red Noses above New Brighton to the steep-sided river valleys of Rivacre; from the open heaths of Caldy Hill to the old, tree-clad cliffs beyond Shotwick castle. What youngster has not, in the ignorance of childhood, plucked these fragile jewels from the stream-banks around Raby Mere – a present for Mum – to arrive home with a sad handful of wilted blooms?

A bluebell wood with its all-pervading colour and scent, on a warm, still day in May is surely one of the finest spectacles of late spring in Wirral.

Peacock butterfly, Thornton Wood

Late spring sees the emergence of the year's first butterflies, some of which will have overwintered by hibernating (perhaps in a dark corner of an attic or roof-space; I recall being shown dozens of dormant red admiral butterflies beneath the dark thatch of an old cottage in Saughall Massie); and some of which will have survived as pupae, to emerge into the warmth of a May day such as this.

The quiet, still clearings in many of Wirral's woods offer warm and sheltered resting- and feeding-places for butterflies, and even at this time of the year it is quite usual to find speckled woods, peacocks, commas and orange-tips.

This peacock butterfly will have spent the long winter months hibernating; its days are now numbered, but its offspring will no doubt be seen in our gardens during late summer and early autumn, flying about the buddleia bushes.

Burton Woods

The village of Burton is sheltered from the easterly winds by the high sandstone ridge whose western slopes are clothed with fine trees. There are many paths running through Burton Woods today, but this was not always so: in the early years of this century a fierce battle arose when a local landowner tried to enclose the woods and keep out the public. Thankfully the public won, and we reap the benefit today.

I love this place, with its mighty old beech trees, sweet chestnuts and sombre pines; the bluebells, ferns and honeysuckle entwining the old tree-trunks; and, hidden amongst the trees, reminders of a bygone age: the falling stones of the old mill and the time-worn, age-weathered Quakers' Graves; and the mellow village church of local red sandstone.

I recall the words of a visitor who wrote about this place whilst walking through the woods many years ago: 'Burton, ever beautiful, is a place to linger in towards evening. Except the softened ring of the anvil towards the end of the village, not a sound comes from the shaded street. Beyond the marshes there is no murmur from the sleeping tide. The note of the woodquest dies in the leafy thickness. Twilight has found you a haunt of ancient peace.'

Great tit, wooded garden

As its name implies, this is the largest member of the tit family, and is common in gardens, woodlands and hedgerows. The nest is a cup of moss and grass lined with down or hair and is normally sited in a hole in a tree-trunk or wall, but the birds also take readily to nest-boxes.

Five to twelve eggs are laid, the young being fed mainly on caterpillars; in fact the birds time their breeding to coincide with the peak numbers of these caterpillars.

Great tits are frequent visitors to bird tables, but they are aggressive and inclined to bully the smaller birds.

Apart from kitchen scraps and peanuts provided by householders the birds consume a variety of food including spring buds, fruits, seeds, berries and spiders.

In autumn and winter the birds roam the countryside in flocks, frequently together with other species.

The beech avenue, Intake Wood, Dibbinsdale

Some of our best habitats are those places where woodland edges adjoin fields and hedgerows, where the trees thin out to let in the light, and the smaller shrubs and bushes – hawthorn, hazel and elder – make ideal homes for our songbirds.

These places are at their best in late spring, when the creamy, heavy-scented flower heads of hawthorn form a lovely backdrop to the wild flowers of our field edges: buttercup, speedwell, stitchwort, campion and bluebells.

I recall a sun-filled day in May, many years ago, at one such place near Neston. It was early morning, and the overnight dew still sparkled in the sunlight. Although early, the sun was already hot, and this sheltered corner was literally humming with life: a myriad of insects danced in the air, several orange-tip butterflies were feeding on the abundant hedge-garlic, and, from the greening woods came the song of a thousand birds. This is spring at its best.

Right: blue tit and hawthorn blossom

Bidston Hill

Wirral's high heathlands show a splash of yellow and green in springtime, as the birch trees burst into leaf and the gorse comes into flower. The sight is especially pleasing on Bidston Hill, that oasis amidst the urbanity of outer Birkenhead.

These wild, rugged heights have for long been the resort of town-weary folk who have appreciated the open spaces, the plants and birds, and the wide-ranging views. Gone, sadly, are the days when the visitor could see from Bidston's summit 'a sea of green, broken here and there by a church, group of cattle, farm-house, or clump of trees, from within which a tiny mere may glisten, and everywhere hedgerows separating the fields, and making them look like garden plots, on all which the light is ever playing, and giving them different shades, almost making them take different forms'.

But these green, rocky, breezy heights are still precious, beautiful – and in the spring of the year, when all is fresh and new, they speak of optimism, of hope for the future, of new life springing up from these ancient, time-worn Wirral stones.

Thurstaston Hill and the Dee Estuary

It had been a day of lowering grey skies, occasional showers and a wild wind blowing in from the west – a typical spring day! All day we had been hoping to get out for a breath of fresh air, for an hour's exercise; but each time we decided to go, the heavens opened and we were forced to stay indoors.

But by seven that evening, as so often happens, the skies in the west started to show breaks in the clouds, the wind dropped a little, and the sun started to show itself, albeit half-heartedly!

Better late than never, we thought, as we set off through the birch-woods of Thurstaston, branches everywhere still dripping after the day's showers, but with an all-pervading, earthy freshness rising from the damp grass and undergrowth. The birds too were seemingly glad to see the fine ending to the day, for the woods resounded to a late evening burst of song after the day's rains.

Thor's Stone seemed gloomy in its confined amphitheatre of bracken and heather, the soft stone dark and saturated with moisture: normally the children would have scrambled to its summit – but not this evening.

Within minutes we were out of those gloomy surroundings and striding the long, stony ridge: that bright, breezy platform above the Dee meadows. On this fine spring evening, the vistas were clear and sharp after the day's showers, the horizons far and wide.

Immediately below us, a blanket of bright gorse swept down towards the shelter-belt of pine trees edging Dawpool Heath; beyond, freshly greening meadows and sprouting hedgerows formed a quilted carpet right up to the Dee's edge. The river itself looked grey and turbulent still, after the day's wet and windy weather; and beyond, under a sky that showed clouds of mauve and patches of blue, the Welsh hills made a low and peaceful backdrop to all that was before us.

We had not long to wait for sunset, when the scene before us was transformed, first to fiery red tints and then to a soft afterglow of pink and purple. Quietly, we headed home, across the dusky heath and through the darkening woods, all of us feeling that the day's wait, the frustrations, had been well repaid in the beautiful experience of the last few hours of this typical spring day in Wirral.

Intake Field and Hindolin Hay, Caldy

Buttercups in a green meadow bordered by unkempt hawthorn hedges, with skylarks singing overhead from a blue sky: such an image is surely the epitome of an English spring, and one which many folk hold dear to their hearts. Our fields, too, present us with a stark reminder of the progression of the seasons, as they change in colour and tone as the year advances.

Wirral's patchwork quilt of fields is a record of man's usage of the land over many hundreds of years; from the earliest times when the first settlers cleared small, irregular enclosures from the woodland and scrubland for their livestock and crops; through the open-field agriculture of strip farming in medieval times and the subsequent periods of Parliamentary Enclosure 200 years ago; to the varied usage of today.

Our meadows today show traces of all these periods of history. I see still, around Wirral's undeveloped villages – Shotwick, Ledsham, Burton – a few small, irregular-shaped fields, their hedgebanks rich in plants which may be relics of ancient woodlands: survivors of a thousand years of land usage.

And in other parts of the peninsula – in

the old townships of Capenhurst, Little Stanney and Irby, I trace the gently curving field boundaries and undulating land-surfaces of medieval ridge and furrow.

From the ridge of Thurstaston Hill I look down on the meadows above the Dee: large, regular, straight-edged fields so typical of the Enclosures of the eighteenth and nineteenth centuries, when the new layouts were planned with pencil and ruler.

Finally, and perhaps sadly, I see around Storeton the fields created by today's land-users: vast, prairie-type landscapes with scarcely a tree or hedgerow in sight. Here, the past has been almost obliterated, save for a few ghost-marks on bare winter soil where an old hedgerow has been grubbed up.

When I take up a tithe map of the 1830s, which lists the field-names and their status, I discover yet another fascinating world, where the fields of a township bear individual personalities: from Three Nook Cake in Wallasey to Twizzle Hay in Raby; from Hungry Hay in Caldy to Yolk of the Egg in Tranmere.

The glory of this season, though, must surely be the profusion of golden-yellow buttercup pastures, from the southernmost parts of the peninsula, at Saughall and Woodbank, to the field-remnants behind Hoylake and West Kirby on the northern coast. These are my spring fields.

Orange-tip butterfly on buttercup, Burton

I always feel that spring has well and truly arrived when I see my first orange-tip of the year. I recall one exceptionally warm March day in Shotwick churchyard, with some three or four of these beautifully coloured butterflies resting on clumps of cuckoo-flower; fleecy clouds scudded across the sun from time to time, and the butterflies opened and closed their wings in response to the changing warmth and light.

The caterpillars of the orange-tip feed on a wide variety of early springtime plants, but prefer the locally common garlic mustard and cuckoo flower.

The intricately patterned underside of the orange-tip's wings provides excellent camouflage, but sadly this lovely insect has a short life of only about eighteen days.

Cowslips, meadow at Meols

We have in Wirral few old meadows, those colourful places where the wild flowers of old grew in profusion. However, between Moreton and Meols, and within a stone's-throw of the sea, a small cluster of fields has survived over-cultivation during recent years, so that today they put forth a fine succession of spring flowers, from the cowslips of April to the ragged robin and ox-eye daisies of May.

I have seen cowslips in one or two other places in Wirral: in Shotwick, and down Brimstage way, but the display on these meadows at Meols is undoubtedly the best. The splash of yellow is unmistakable even from afar, and closer inspection reveals large clumps and smaller clusters of flowers, scattered about the meadows.

After the cowslips have finished, the meadows burst into bloom as spring rushes into summer: speedwells, meadowsweet, ragged robin, ox-eye daisies, orchids, knapweed, and others. And with the flowers come the butterflies: in a good year, clouds of meadow-browns, small coppers, common blues, gatekeepers. A truly wonderful place.

Left: Spring wild flowers at Dibbinsdale

Ponds, Wirral Country Park, Thurstaston

Some of my earliest – and fondest – childhood memories are of long days spent by a pond which, to me and my friends, was a particularly magical place. Black Harry's, we called it – it was right by the railway line in Moreton – and after school we would dash to its bare and baked bank to catch a few stickleback and tadpoles or just play hide-and-seek amongst the blackthorn bushes around its edge.

Black Harry's has long gone – filled in, like so many of Wirral's old ponds and pits – and with it the memories, the wildlife, the plants, the bushes, the butterflies and dragonflies, the birds – and the *wildness*.

Happily, Wirral still has an abundance of ponds, each with its own unique character, each in its own special setting, each a small, self-contained world of life and colour, a rich tapestry of plants and birds, amphibians, mammals and insects.

Even a cursory glance at a large-scale map of the Wirral Peninsula shows, within the network of fields and hedgerows, a huge number of ponds and pits – perhaps as many as one or more per field in some parts. In some fields they are grouped in small clusters of three or four together, and some straddle the hedge-boundaries of two adjoining fields. Most of these ponds are quite regular in shape and often square.

So much for the maps, but what we see on the ground is a rich diversity indeed. Many ponds are overgrown with vegetation: grasses, shrubs and even trees cloak and choke the ponds, so that from a short distance they look not like a pond but more like a small wooded copse. Some have been, or are in the process of being, in-filled – ponds and pits make a convenient dumping-ground for unwanted rubble!

Some very few are what we all would wish to see in a real, living pond: a couple of thorn hedges, perhaps, growing on the bank; a shallow, damp area where marsh-loving plants will thrive; and a deeper stand of water towards the centre, encircling a small island.

Such ponds do exist, usually deliberately managed by a local landowner or amenity group – perhaps for their fishing, or for their wildlife value. In late spring, these ponds are at their best, their waters and environs vibrant with new life:

tadpoles undergoing their miraculous transformation; wildfowl feeding chicks; water-plants sprouting new shoots and flower-buds; damsel-flies mating; and early swallows diving low for insects.

Most of Wirral's ponds were originally dug out as marl-pits, a practice which had its origins at least five hundred years ago. We know from old documents that during the reign of Edward I about seventy marl-pits were dug around Wirral by Abbot Simon – at Bromborough, Irby, Eastham, Sutton, Childer Thornton and Whitby.

Marl is a lime-like substance which lies in pockets below the surface of the ground, and the practice of marling in Cheshire was described in Tudor times:

' . . . they use for manure a kind of blue marble-like earth which they call marl. This is an excellent manure, and though it be exceeding chargeable, yet through good neighbourhood it quiteth the cost; for if you manure your grounds once in seven or twelve years it is sufficient, and look how many years he beareth corn, so many he will bear grass, and that plenty.'

Getting the marl out of the ground and subsequently spreading it over the adjacent fields was not an easy task; neither was it cheap. The pockets of marl had first to be found, then a gang of marlers would set to work in extracting the marl. Many old marl-pits today still bear the characteristic

slope at one end, where the loaded carts were drawn out; the opposite end is usually sharply cut, where the marl was dug out from the field.

Once abandoned, most of the old pits gradually filled with water, for the clayey soil made an excellent, impervious base through which rain-water could not escape.

Today, these reminders of a bygone age lie widely distributed across the Wirral countryside. Left to nature's own devices, their natural progression is to gradually silt up as each season's detritus of falling leaves, grasses and twigs accumulates, making the ponds shallower as the years go by. Trees and shrubs, self-sown by wind-blown or bird-carried seeds, take root in and around the pond. These in turn absorb the little remaining water and encourage further accumulation of leaf-litter, until the pit is no more.

Unless, of course, some kindly individual or group comes along and rescues the pond from its sad fate, transforming it into a living sanctuary for water wildlife in all its rich variety . . .

Heron, Gilroy Nature Park, West Kirby

7am on a fine spring morning. This wetland area at the edge of West Kirby is an oasis for wild creatures whose focus is the fine sheet of water at the edge of the fields.

The pond at this early hour is already busy: a family of mallard with its entourage of a dozen chicks forages around the reeds at the water's edge looking for food. A Canada goose alights noisily on the water, sending arcs of spray across the pond and disturbing a moorhen going otherwise unconcernedly about his early-morning business. A fox slinks quietly through the bushes from a late-night foray in the local gardens, to curl up in a safe, hidden corner of the field. In the distance a lone cuckoo sends its call across the meadows.

Aloof from all the activity, a lone heron stands motionless in the shadows, waiting with infinite patience for a fish to come within range of its dagger-sharp bill. The strike is lightning-fast as the bill plunges into the water emerging, more often than not, with the fish firmly grasped, and, if small enough, swallowed whole.

Canada goose, Gilroy Nature Park

Wirral's ponds are mostly small: fine for many water-loving creatures, but not really adequate for some of the larger water-birds with large wing-spans who need plenty of room to manoeuvre. Such birds will prefer the larger sheets of water such as the lake at Thornton Manor where a number of pairs of Canada geese breed. At Gilroy Nature Park in West Kirby one or two pairs nest each year.

These birds were introduced into Britain in the seventeenth century and have spread widely since. They will settle anywhere where there are large lakes or ponds, even in town centres. On such waters there is constant activity with birds frequently taking off and landing accompanied by their loud 'honking' calls.

Birds pair for life and build their nests on the ground near water; the chicks leave the nest on hatching but are reliant on their parents who protect them against predators for several weeks.

Sedge warbler, Gilroy Nature Park

When we think of ponds, we usually think of the creatures that live in or on the water – the frogs, toads, insects, water-birds – but many of Wirral's ponds have good shrubbery adjacent to the water. These provide excellent nesting places for small birds, who will also find insect life in abundance on and around the water.

The sedge warbler is a summer visitor, arriving from mid-May; when it first arrives it sings night and day with an incessant chatter of varying tones. It nests low down in the dense waterside vegetation, building a deep cup of grasses and sedges; the young are fed on insects such as damsel-flies and aphids. The bird is found in those parts of Wirral with good cover beside ponds and ditches.

Common frog, suburban garden pond

Suburban ponds are beneficial to frogs as an important substitute for the decline in numbers of ponds in the countryside. Frogs spend much of their time on land, but in early spring they will gather to spawn, with all the eggs being laid usually within a few days. Tadpoles hatch after two to three weeks and then take about three months to develop into tiny frogs.

Dew-covered damsel-fly on waterside stem

This tiny damsel-fly, only about one-and-a-quarter inches long, has spent the night clinging to a stem and is now covered in dew; it will not be able to fly until the sun has dried the moisture from its wings. As with dragon-flies, damsel-flies spend the early part of their lives under water as larvae which emerge after a year when the mature insect breaks free of the larval skin.

Pond, Wirral Country Park, Thurstaston

As spring becomes summer, the plant-life of Wirral's ponds grows tall and lush, and many water-loving plants come into flower: water-lilies, reedmace, meadowsweet, water crowfoot, arrow-head, and the colourful purple loosestrife.

As the water warms up, tadpoles change to tiny frogs and, after a damp spell of weather, emerge from the water en masse, to be seen jumping about in the long, wet grass on the pond-bank.

There is always something to see, something of interest, beside our ponds at this, the height of the season. Often the life of the pond is hidden, unseen: only an undercurrent of activity, a succession of subdued sounds, indicates the wealth of life which is being enacted out in the reeds, deep in the undergrowth, or beneath the surface of the water.

Insects and birds come and go, resting for a while perhaps on the tall stems of the reedmace, or taking a drink at the water's edge; damsel-flies and, perhaps, an early dragon-fly, flit across the water's surface; and small mammals rustle in the decaying leaf-litter of last autumn. This is nature at its richest.

49

Spring wild flowers, Red Rocks Marsh

This delightful place by the Dee Estuary, right on the north-western tip of Wirral, starts to come alive in late spring, when the first of a long succession of unique and fascinating plants come into flower. One of the earliest is star-of-bethlehem *(below)*, a very uncommon plant which flourishes on the dunes behind the marsh; but the glory of springtime is the yellow flag iris *(left)* which grows in the open wet areas.

Natterjack toad, Red Rocks Marsh

Apart from the few early flowering plants of spring the most unusual feature of this fascinating marsh at the edge of the sea is surely the rare natterjack toad.

Walk along the boardwalk from West Kirby to Red Rocks on warm, still evenings in May, and you may be lucky enough to experience the amazing sound of the male toads calling to the females. Unless experienced at first-hand, this sound is quite unbelievable: a vibrating, cackling, resonant sound which, when uttered by several males together, can be heard as far away as a mile in the right conditions.

The colony at Red Rocks is the only remaining colony in Wirral, and there are even doubts as to its present status, for numbers of breeding natterjacks seem to have declined in recent years.
T. A. Coward, the great Cheshire naturalist, wrote around the turn of the century about natterjacks in Wirral:

'In the 1880s and early 1890s the natterjack was abundant on the Wallasey sandhills, frequenting the shallow pools in the hollows amongst the dunes. When these sandhills were converted into golf-links most of these pools were drained. On several occasions recently we failed to discover a single natterjack at Wallasey, but on the low-lying land behind the Leasowe Embankment it is still abundant. In 1854, one was taken between Egremont and New Brighton, and in 1851 at Oxton Hill.'

The toads can be easily recognised by the distinctive yellow stripe down their back, and by their strings of spawn, which are shorter than those of the common toad.

It is not known why the natterjacks are disappearing from Red Rocks, but its migratory habits are well known: the naturalist Bell, writing 150 years ago, states that the natterjack, once so common in his garden, had lately abandoned it. 'For some years past,' he writes, 'not one has been seen, and no cause has ever suggested itself for its disappearance.'

Thrift on Middle Hilbre

It had been a rather miserable week – a typical spell of May weather, perhaps: cloudy skies and cold winds from the north-west, with frequent heavy showers. Saturday morning though dawned clear and bright: the air absolutely sparkled with spring freshness, and the sun shone from a cloudless sky. The light breeze came from the northern quarter, cool but clear: a good day for Hilbre and its springtime show of thrift!

The sands between West Kirby and Hilbre were still wet from the ebbing tide, and sparkled in the morning sunlight. The sea horizons were clear and wide, and the Welsh hills seemed so near as to be able to touch them. The air was fresh and sweet: so pure it almost hurt to breathe in too deeply.

As we approached the middle isle, we sensed already the glory that was to come: a splash of pink about the cliff-edges and stony outcrops, and gaining the cliff-top we were not disappointed. It was a good year for Hilbre's display of thrift: the winter's salt-laden sprays and land-lashing waves had encouraged this riotous display of colour that stretched before us as far as we could see. A carpet of pink along the western edge, mingled here and there with the deeper colour of bluebells and the pale green of sprouting bracken fronds.

We could scarcely put one foot in front of the other for fear of treading upon this carpet of thrift, so densely packed were the plants. Great clumps cascaded over the cliff-edge, its colour blending with the soft pink of the sandstone.

There was so much else to see, to do, on this beautiful spring day: in the distance the seals sent forth their haunting cry across the sandbanks of the estuary; there were caves to explore, rock-pools in which to paddle, and – best of all – a packed lunch to enjoy later, relaxing on the soft warm turf.

These isles in the Dee Estuary are many things to many people: to some, they are a place from which to view the flocks of wading-birds and sea-birds which visit the estuary in spring, autumn and winter; to others, they are a place to which they can escape every so often, to refresh weary spirits and enjoy the vastnesses of sand, sea and sky.

To us, on that beautiful day in late spring, the Hilbre Isles were flower-bedecked jewels in the mouth of the Dee. Surely enough, we would return to this sanctuary in the sea – in summer, perhaps, when the purple rock-sea lavender is in full flower, and the white campion brightens the green turf. Or in autumn, to witness the amassing wader-flocks as they head southwards to warmer climes for the cold months to follow. And in deepest winter, when frost enshrouds the dead bracken-fronds, and icicles drape the eastern cliff-crags.

But whatever our future joys and wonders to be experienced in this lovely place, the memories of this May day, with its blue skies, gentle breezes, pure air, and the rich tapestry of nature's blossoming, would last for ever as one of life's great experiences.

Spring sunset over the Dee Estuary and Hilbre

During wintertime, the sun sets over the Welsh hills when seen from Wirral lands, but as the year creeps on, the sun sets each day a little more to the north, and by springtime it is clear of the hills of Wales and sinks instead seemingly into the waters of the Irish Sea.

Wirral sunsets are renowned for their beauty, particularly when seen from West Kirby or the hills above that town. I have seen, in my lifetime, sunsets from many places from within and outside this land of ours: over mountains and hills, over forests and moors, and over seas far from here. But I have yet to see a sunset compare with those that we see on a spring evening as the sun sinks low over the Dee Estuary.

On no two evenings are the sunsets alike: on one occasion, following an Atlantic depression with its associated rain, perhaps, the sky will be a bright yellow, the sun obscured by fleecy clouds which turn a greeny-orange as the sun lowers to the horizon. On the following evening, the sun is red-orange in a hazy, grey-blue sky as an intense anticyclone sets in over the country.

The sunsets change, too, with the state of the tides over the estuary: high, rough tides seem to absorb the light, whilst low tides and vast expanses of wet sand reflect the light back to the sky, giving dramatic effects in the direction of the setting sun.

Some of the most beautiful experiences of my life have been those spring evenings when walking homewards after a day on Hilbre: the lowering sun sinking towards the far-off sea; light clouds over mainland Wirral glowing pink as they catch the dying orb's rays; landwards, the first lights of West Kirby lighting up the deepening gloom; and, away across the estuary, the haunting, echoing cries of a flock of oyster-catchers winging across the wet sands.

Summer

Pond, Realey's Field, Thurstaston

'I CANNOT leave it; I must stay under the old tree in the midst of the long grass, the luxury of the leaves, and the song in the very air. I seem as if I could feel all the glowing life the sunshine gives and the south wind calls to being. The endless grass, the endless leaves, the immense strength of the oak expanding, the unalloyed joy of finch and blackbird; from all of them I receive a little. Each gives me something of the pure joy they gather for themselves.'

Thus wrote Richard Jefferies of summer a hundred years ago. Here was a man who was close to nature, close to the earth's seasons; a man who felt himself to be a very part of creation. In our times this feeling of being one with nature comes to us rarely: we have too many distractions, we are too tied to the artificial world of the twentieth century. But occasionally we may, like Jefferies, on a summer's day – lying in a sweet meadow under a blue sky, perhaps, or walking in the soft stillness of a June evening – know that unity we have with our natural world.

In the depths of winter – when we see death and decay all around us, when the twigs are black and bare, when the grass is yellow and dank, when the earth is brown and barren – we cannot imagine that the richness of summer will ever return to Wirral. My favourite images of summer –

of skylarks trilling high above the Dee meadows, of a soft west wind rustling the branches of great oaks in our woods, of butterflies dancing on purple knapweed, of golden sunsets across the estuary – seem part of another world, another planet. But come they do, every year, as unerringly as the night turns to day; the promise of spring becomes the full-blooded climax of nature's very purpose. But this season we call summer has beginnings and endings that are poles apart.

How fresh are its beginnings, those soft days of late May and early June when spring becomes summer, when the raiment of the trees is a soft green, when the bird-song is still eager and jubilant, when the flowers are bright and complement the freshness of the grass and the softness of the earth. There is a newness in the very air, in the breeze that sweeps towards our small peninsula from Welsh uplands and vast oceans away to the west.

Yet how quickly does this part of the season go by! By late June the greens are becoming darker: the elder blossoms, the last display of whiteness in our hedgerows, are withering to brown, and the hawthorn hedges are already displaying small berries, the creamy blossoms of May now just a distant memory. Nature is now at its richest, our lane-sides, meadows and hedgerows a lush tangle of long grasses and wild-flowers. How exquisite are these long midsummer evenings and, in these northern latitudes, how bright the skies at midnight on those clear nights when a cool, northerly airstream settles over our land. There arises from the countryside on

Left: Hybrid orchids, Moreton

Right: Foxgloves, Thornton Wood, Raby Mere

such evenings a mixture of nature's perfumes that no man-made pot-pourri could match: of wild-rose and honeysuckle, of lime-blossoms and pine-sap.

But already the bird-song has softened to a shadow of its Maytime exuberance: the call of the cuckoo has died away, the estuaries and shores are quiet now after the earlier influx of wading-birds; and the magic of the woodlands in spring has turned to a drab tangle of rampant bramble-stems.

By now, the weather-pattern for the summer has usually declared itself. Probably an Atlantic-dominated season, with frequent, rain-bearing weather systems coming in from the west, with short, fine spells in between. These, to my mind, are the best summers. The temperatures are pleasantly moderate, the rain keeps the landscape looking green and lush, and the air is fresh and clear. Bad for butterflies and barbecues, but good for the constitution and the garden!

Some years, though, anticyclonic weather dominates, with a stubborn high-pressure system feeding hot, dry, dusty air in from the continental east. Such years are remembered for their long spells of hot, dry, settled weather; we still talk about the summer of '76, with its plagues of ladybirds and its hosepipe bans. In such conditions the landscape becomes drab and lifeless: green turns to yellow under a cloudless, featureless sky; trees and plants wilt in the scorching temperatures; and the interminable heat-haze makes one long day follow another in endless succession. We often in Wirral escape the drenching thunderstorms that drift up from the continent, and the earth continues to bake. Only the insects appreciate the conditions, and such summers make superb 'butterfly years'.

Usually, though, by July and into August summer is past its best; already there is a hint of the coming autumn as hedgerow fruits start to ripen and flowers turn to seed; the pastoral landscape changes as crops ripen and are gathered, and the varied hues of early-summer green become a monotone drabness. The sun, which has been setting in the sea on Wirral's northern horizon, comes ever so

Left: Male common blue butterfly, Red Rocks Marsh

Right: Mistle thrush

gradually round to sink behind the estuary, and often delivers a grand sunset spectacle for evening strollers on Wirral's western shores at Hoylake and West Kirby.

This season, that such a short time ago seemed so young and fresh, so endless, is already showing signs of old age. Already the swifts and swallows are gathering together, to leave soon for lands where there is summer all the year round. Already the first leaves are withering on the trees. Only around the coast, on the dunes and on the marshes, are the plants still new: at Red Rocks the sea-holly is coming into purple flower, the burnet rose is wearing creamy-white blooms, and the sea-aster bedecks the endless marsh at Parkgate.

On early mornings in late August there is already an autumnal feel to the air, a heavy dew on the grass, a chill that heralds another change in the annual cycle of nature's seasons; and by September – although we may experience days of summer-like weather – the best is over, and the year is growing old.

But as Jefferies says, 'Let the shadow advance upon the dial – I can watch it with equanimity while it is there to be watched. It is only when the shadow is not there, when the clouds of winter cover it, that the dial is terrible. The invisible shadow goes on and steals from us. But now, while I can see the shadow of the tree and watch it slowly gliding across the grass, it is mine. These are the only hours that are not wasted – these hours that absorb the soul and fill it with beauty. The hours when the mind is absorbed by beauty are the only hours when we really live, so that the longer we can stay among these things so much the more is snatched from inevitable Time.'

Early summer flowers, meadow at Meols

Early June: a warm sun shines from a blue sky studded with fleecy-white clouds, with just a gentle breeze to keep body temperatures comfortable. The gentle rains of late spring have been a welcome tonic to this rather dry coastal strip between the railway and the embankment, and the plants and grasses of the few remnant meadows have blossomed forth as a result.

The cowslips of mid-spring have finished – just a few dried seed-heads remain to show their former presence – and the short-lived may-blossom of these wind-blown hedgerows is but a memory. Just about now, though, these meadows are coming into their best, as the mainstream summer plants come into flower.

The delicate pink flowers of ragged robin – also called bachelor's buttons, from the days when country girls used the plant to identify their future husband – stand tall in the damper corners of the meadows; and the bright yellow-rattle, whose dried seed-heads really do rattle in the breeze, forms large patches in the drier parts. In some parts of the land farmers would use the rattling sound as a signal that the time was right for haymaking.

As this lovely fresh June breeze sends ripples across the carpet of grasses, the white flower-heads of ox-eye daisies dance about like lights in the night, shaking off the early summer butterflies and bees. The meadows on such a day have a restless, almost lifelike feel: nothing is still, all of nature is alive to the season.

Only in the wet gullies which separate the meadows will there be quiet pockets which the interminable breeze cannot touch: little havens of stillness where reeds and rushes play host to dragon-flies and damsel-flies, and where flourishes the meadowsweet, its rich creamy flower-heads still in bud.

This is a place too for other summer creatures: swifts and swallows perch ten-in-a-row on the trackside telegraph wires; skylarks call clearly from seemingly miles above; and from far away, from a distant hedgerow, comes the monotonous call of the cuckoo.

Occasionally, when the wind abates for a few brief seconds, one hears the restless sound of waves breaking on the wet sands, and the faint calling of sea-birds; but these sounds are so faint, so short-lived, that one has perhaps imagined them – perhaps it was just the sound of the breeze rustling through the reeds and grasses.

Right: Azure damsel-fly on knapweed

Common spotted orchid hybrids, near Clatterbridge

Of all the summer flowers, the orchids must surely rank amongst the top favourites. I well remember my first conscious appreciation of these special plants: of stumbling upon a solitary spike in a corner of an otherwise ordinary field where we played rowdy games of tick and hide & seek. I told no one of this flower: it was my secret, my plant. Each day after school I sneaked a look at this precious bloom glowing majestically in my secret corner.

Whether or not it flowered in successive summers I do not know, for my mind had by then turned to other interests. Probably not, knowing the fickleness of orchids. Plants that flourish one year vanish without trace the next, so that one is left wondering whether the sighting was an illusion.

But their very unpredictability, perhaps, is part of their beauty, their mystique. For one never knows where they might turn up next. And they do choose the most unlikely places to flourish. In Moreton, for example, the meadows by the railway line, looked after as a nature reserve, have a few orchids, but nothing spectacular; yet on the other side of the line, in the remnants of an old field left by the builders after completing a new housing estate, they flourish: myriads of stately, pink flowers, blooming adjacent to the rubbish and rubble!

There used to be more orchids in Wirral than there are now. A hundred years ago a handbook of Wirral flowers said that the pyramidal orchid was found 'among the sandhills at Wallasey'; the green-winged orchid 'on Oxton heath, Moreton to West Kirby, Raby, Hooton, Willaston, Shotwick'; the fragrant orchid 'in Upton, Langfields West Kirby, Leasowe, Arrowe'; the frog orchid 'near Grange landmark, Theobauld's field, Bidston Hill'; and the lesser butterfly orchid 'at Eastham, Bebington, Sutton, north side of Bromborough Pool, Hilbre, Barnston'.

Today, the common spotted orchid predominates locally; however, much hybridisation takes place, particularly, it is believed, with the southern marsh orchid, and plants can appear which show characteristics of the different types. But whatever their names, all of our orchids are rare, beautiful plants to be nurtured and cherished in whatever way we are able.

Bee orchid, near Clatterbridge

One hundred years ago there were no records of the bee orchid having been seen in Wirral, but it has appeared, scattered and sporadic, in one or two places in the peninsula in recent years.

This beautiful and fascinating plant is unmistakable in appearance, and strange in action. The lip of the flower mimics a female bumble-bee: this is to attract a male bee which will try to mate with it. As it lands on the flower lip, pollen becomes attached to its head, but when the bee finds no response from the 'female' it flies on to another flower, so cross-pollinating the flower.

However, in Britain this complicated set-up is not needed because the plants pollinate themselves before the bee lands.

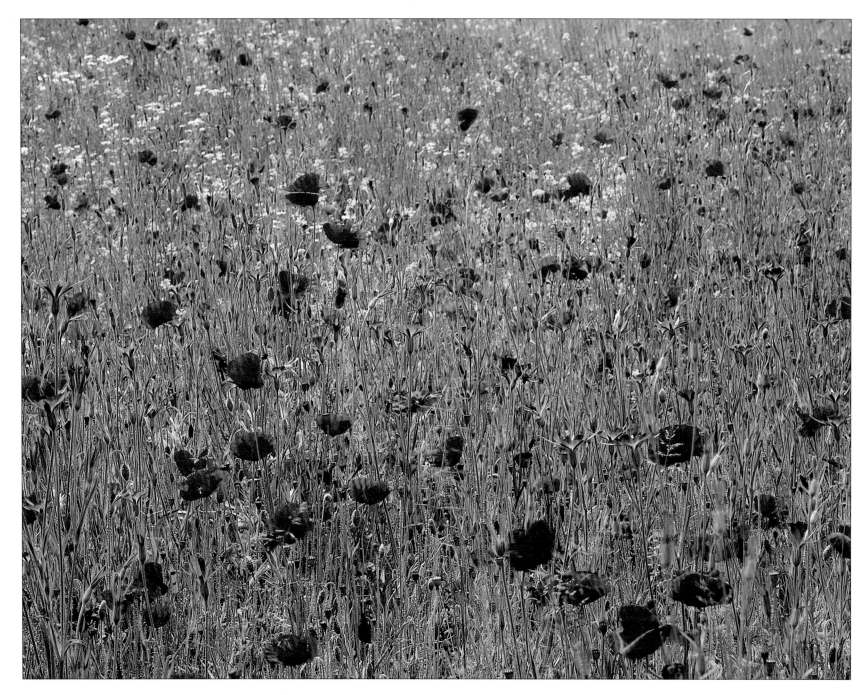

Wild flowers, walled garden, Royden Park, Frankby

Scenes such as this are rare in our rural landscapes today, as farming practices have eliminated the unwanted 'weeds' through the use of selective weedkillers and cleaner seeds.

Poppies, though, have a habit of appearing in the most unlikely of places, particularly where land has been disturbed, and some of our best summer flowerscapes are after the completion of roadworks or building works; before the landscape contractors come along and prettify the scene, nature often puts on its own show, with a dazzling display of field poppies.

Such plants, along with others like corncockle and scabious, also survive in field-corners and edges, where the land remains in a semi-cultivated state. Perhaps, with the trend towards less intensive use of our agricultural land, we may yet again see scenes such as this to add colour and life to our otherwise green, monotone farmlands.

Small skipper butterfly, Wirral Way

Years ago, the skippers were not very common in Wirral, but recent years have seen an increase in numbers, so that they are now quite numerous.

They are easy to identify when resting on a flower-head, for they hold the fore-wings partially raised and the hind-wings horizontal in a typical skipper-type fashion. They are often aggressive too in their defence of territory, making sudden flights to intercept passing insects, including other skippers. They prefer areas of long grass with a good assortment of wild flowers such as thistles and knapweed.

Sunrise over Montgomery Hill, Frankby

Midsummer: the sun rises over the Wirral countryside after the shortest night of the year to reveal a misty morn that heralds another fine day in a spell of settled weather. Even at this early hour the wildlife of the countryside is stirring: the rooks are flying towards their feeding-grounds for the day, to return perhaps in twelve hours' time towards sunset; rabbits come forth from their burrows to feed and play on the dew-laden grass; and the foxes and badgers return to their subterranean homes after a night's foraging excursion.

Right: Small skipper butterflies waiting for the sun to dry the morning dew from their wings

Comma butterfly, Rivacre Valley

Another success story! In former times this fine-looking insect was rarely seen in Wirral, but it is now quite common. Easily recognised by its ragged wings with distinct white 'comma' mark beneath, the butterfly is a rather solitary creature and spends its time in a small area with brambles, nettles, thistles and knapweed.

Common blue butterfly, Wirral Way

Walk along the boardwalk at Red Rocks Marsh, or along parts of the Wirral Way during hot days in July and August, and you are almost certain to see this delicate little butterfly. Where it is seen, there are usually quite a lot: I have counted eight or nine in a small area of just a few square yards in good summers. It is the male who has the irridescent wing-markings that glisten in the summer sunlight – the females are a softer brown colour. There can be fewer sights more lovely than seeing these fine butterflies fluttering about the summer flowers on a bright sunny day.

Rabbit, Thurstaston Common

Late on a fine summer's evening on any open rough grassy space in Wirral one is almost certain to spot a family of rabbits playing or nibbling the stems and stalks of grasses and flowers.

Some country folk tend to dislike them on account of the damage they may cause to crops; townsfolk love them for the gentle and cuddly image portrayed in story-books.

Rabbits have been with us for a long time: they were introduced from the continent in the twelfth century as a source of food and for their skins, and their populations have fluctuated over the years as diseases have taken their toll. However, their notorious breeding habits soon make up any shortfall in numbers, and populations rise quickly after decimation.

The evidence for a large rabbit population in Wirral over the centuries is clear in the large number of field-names which refer to rabbits in their old name of coney: 'Coney Hay', 'Coney Greaves' and 'Warren Hay' are field-names which all indicate an association of that part of the township with rabbits.

Despite the damage caused to much vegetation by these creatures, they do have their benefits in some parts of our landscape, for they nibble the grass to give a short, almost close-mown surface which encourages the growth of the low-growing and creeping plants such as vetches and trefoils which would otherwise be crowded out by the stronger, denser vegetation.

But, like them or not, the common bunnies, with their associated burrows and warrens, and short-cropped turf, are likely to be a feature of our landscape and countryside for a long time to come.

Fox, near Caldy

10.30pm on a fine summer's night: in this quiet corner of a Caldy field the gentle dusk is gathering, the activity and the sounds of daytime are dying away. A few birds make late songs, but otherwise all is quiet and still. Then, unannounced, quite unconcernedly and with a hint of arrogance, a fox emerges from the hedgerow, its senses alert after a day's rest curled up in some warm, hidden corner.

It is time for action, time to search out food from man's and nature's rich store of offerings. Tonight this slinky creature will forage in suburban and town gardens, amongst compost-heaps and around farms, for scraps that will nourish and fill. In the countryside foxes will catch small mammals and beetles, and in autumn feed on fruit.

He will for the most part be a sleuth of the darkness, a ghost in the night. We may catch a glimpse of him in our headlamps as we drive home; we may be awakened by his raucous call in the depths of the night. But we will never get really close to the fox, for he will always be one step ahead.

The history of foxes in Wirral is interesting. So used are we today to seeing them in abundant numbers right across the peninsula, in town, suburb and country, that it is difficult to believe that at the turn of the century Coward described the fox as 'now scarce in Wirral'; and Neilson wrote in the 30s that 'nowadays Reynard is rather a rarity in the peninsula, though as recently as 1929 one entered Bidston Village'.

During Victorian times, however, foxes flourished in Wirral, as is evidenced by the graphic accounts of the fox-hunting fraternity of those days:

'Storeton and Prenton covers and woods were well stocked with foxes in the old hunting days . . . Squire Webster of Upton Hall had near his residence many fine covers and plantations with good lying for foxes . . . in my youth Bidston Hill Wood and cover, Noctorum, Aspinall's Gorse, and Gillbrook Woods were complete nurseries for foxes. I may say the same of Oxton, Prenton and Storeton Woods' (Henry K. Aspinall, 1903).

Fox-hunting was carried on as early as the thirteenth century, but took off in earnest in Victorian times, with the settling in the area of men of wealth and with spare time, and the creation of large private estates.

Others too wished to see the riddance of foxes; many parish church registers tell of the payment, during the 1700s and 1800s, for the killing of foxes, for many folk regarded them as 'a sincere pest'.

Today, they are everywhere. Foxes regularly forage along the shorelines, and frequently cross the wet sands of the Dee Estuary to Hilbre – sometimes getting caught by the tide, if the evidence of foxes washed up on our beaches is anything to go by! However, their future seems assured by their versatility and resourcefulness.

Pond, Wirral Country Park, Thurstaston

By the middle of summer, the life of our ponds has reached its zenith. The plant-life is in full flower: water-lilies are at their best, purple loosestrife is putting on a magnificent display, and the pondside shrubs are in full leaf. On a warm, still day the air above the pond is alive with insect life of all kinds: gnats and midges hover, damsel-flies rest on the reed-stalks, dragon-flies flit from stem to stem, and small birds hop about in the bushes, foraging for the best food in this wealth of abundance.

Supported on the surface, pond-skaters seek out insects which fall on to the water. Small newts and frogs, newly developed from tadpoles, are emerging to explore their new-found world; whilst in the depths the cycle of life and death continues as the larvae of dragon-flies and diving-beetles seek out their prey.

Common frog

Frogs have many predators and have few natural defences, especially when they are out of water. However, they are able to jump with startling rapidity; the back legs can be extended fully within one-tenth of a second. When danger approaches, the frog will often plunge into the depths of the pond for safety, or jump towards the nearest protective cover.

Southern hawker dragon-fly

The eggs of the dragon-fly are laid in the water of ponds and develop into larvae which spend up to two years under water preying on insects, tadpoles and small fish. When the time has come for the dragon-fly to emerge, the larva crawls up a reed-stem early on a summer morning. The skin on the back of the larva splits and the dragonfly emerges. Over the next few hours the wings unfold from their crumpled state and the body gradually extends to its full length. The photograph shows the empty skin-case of the larva with the dragon-fly almost fully developed and ready to fly.

Heathers, Thurstaston Common

By late summer the Wirral countryside generally is looking rather flat and uninteresting: the trees have assumed a tired, dark-green look, the hedgerow blossoms and wayside flowers are finished. But summer still has a final show of colour to display on our heathlands, in the glorious purples of our heathers and the yellows of our late-flowering gorse.

Wirral's heaths – Bidston Hill, Heswall Dales, Grange and Caldy Hills, Thurstaston Common and Irby Heath – moorland areas that for much of the year appear drab and lifeless, grey and uninteresting, suddenly come ablaze with colour in July and August, as these wonderful plants come into bloom for a brief but beautiful period.

We are lucky to have in Wirral all three flowering heathers: cross-leaved heath, bell heather and ling. The cross-leaved heath is usually the first to flower. Its leaves are grey-green, and form a cross when seen from above. It is unusual too in preferring the damper hollows of our commons, whereas the other heathers prefer the drier parts.

Right: Small tortoiseshell on bell heather

As the cross-leaved heath finishes flowering, so the succession of colour is continued by the coming into flower of the bell heather and ling. All heathers have adapted themselves to exist in poor soils, and there can be few soils poorer than on these high, windswept, sandy ridges, where the porous sandstone quickly soaks up rainwater and nutrients.

The heathers have been used over the years by man, as fuel for fires, to make brushes and brooms, to fashion baskets, for thatching, and as bedding material.

Many butterflies and moths love these heathlands, and sometimes clouds of small moths will rise in the air as a walker disturbs their resting-places on the heather plants.

Our heathlands are, surprisingly, not 'natural' areas: the tendency is for these places to eventually become woodland, as can be clearly seen on many of Wirral's heaths where no control has been exercised over the colonisation by birch, pines, and oak trees. Old photos of Bidston Hill and Thurstaston Common show few trees, for

the extensive grazing of those days helped prevent the commons from maturing to woodland. Today, much effort is put into maintaining the open nature of Wirral's heaths, by removing birch and pine seedlings and by experimenting with sheep-grazing.

I can think of no better place to walk than over Thurstaston Hill on a fine August morning, with just a hint of autumn in the air and a heavy overnight dew forming droplets on those fine gossamer-like webs that decorate and lace the heather plants and gorse bushes. Away below the high ridge the meadows by the Dee rise out of the mist which hides the river, and from far, far away comes the soft sound of a myriad wading-birds foraging on the wet sands of the estuary for food to see them on their long, forthcoming journey home to the South.

Left: Dew-covered spider's web on late-summer vegetation

Right: Late summer on Thurstaston Common

Cottongrass, Kitty's Flash, Thurstaston Common

Years ago, our heathlands and commons were wetter than they are today, and these conditions encouraged the growth of plants such as the cottongrass, which prefers the boggy hollows of which a few still remain on Bidston Hill and Thurstaston Common.

This is a strange and unmistakable plant, for its fluffy white flower-heads can be seen from a distance, dancing in the breeze.

Such was its abundance in former times that local folk used to collect arms-full of cottongrass to stuff mattresses, pillows and eiderdowns, and candle-wicks could be formed from the cotton-like strands of the flower-heads.

Bog asphodel, Thurstaston Common

A few other plants thrive in the damper areas of our commons, bog asphodel being one of the prettiest. This yellow-starred flower is rare in Wirral, but a few flower-heads survive on Thurstaston Common.

The plant's name derives from the Latin for 'bone-breaking', for it was once thought that the plant was responsible for brittleness in the bones of animals that ate it. In some parts of the country, maidens used to use the flower-heads to make a yellow dye, which they used for colouring their hair, hence the local name of maiden hair.

Another interesting plant of these damp, boggy places is the sundew, a few plants of which survive on Wirral heaths. The sundew feeds on insects which are trapped on the sticky leaves; it is claimed that a single plant can catch as many as 2,000 insects in a season!

Great spotted woodpecker

The male bird can be distinguished by the red nape patch which the female lacks, although she does have the red area under the tail. These woodpeckers are quite common in our woodlands and will visit suitable garden bird-tables.

Left: Thurstaston Common

Below: Many-zoned polypore, a small bracket fungus which can be found throughout the year, here growing on a heathland birch stump together with mosses and lichens

Foxgloves, Thurstaston Hill

A still, warm, sunny evening at the height of summer: the sun's rays streaming through the trees at the woodland edge catch a solitary foxglove plant, highlighting flowers and leaves. It is unusual to find a single plant like this, for where foxgloves grow, one usually finds many others en masse.

I love this stately plant, which we always equate with the long, warm days around midsummer. In fact the plant is a veritable measure of the season's progress, for the number of bells left flowering towards the top of the stem gives some indication of the advance of summer.

Foxgloves, like poppies, seem to thrive where the earth has been disturbed. I see old badger-setts, where the soil has been heaped into huge bare banks, aglow with the plant a year or two after the badgers have left the place for new territory. For a season the foxgloves smother the ground with colour – shades of pink, with a hint of white – from seeds that have perhaps lain dormant for years. Subsequent years may see one or two plants, but never the majesty of the first year's blooms.

Speckled wood butterfly, Storeton Woods

Many years ago this attractive butterfly was described as being rarely seen in Wirral, but it is now common in most parts of the peninsula.

Its rather insignificant wing-colourings make the speckled wood blend in nicely in its preferred habitat of open clearings in woods or on overgrown hedgerows and now also in many suburban gardens. With dappled sunlight on its wings, the speckled wood seems to be a natural part of the bramble bushes on which it likes to rest.

Badger and sett, West Wirral

A warm, still, evening in the grounds of a large old house somewhere in West Wirral. In an overgrown, wild, wooded corner, amidst a tangle of brambles and ivy, something is astir. The piles of out-thrown earth, heaps of grass bedding and gaping holes are the distinctive clues to the occupants of this secluded corner of Wirral, and, sure enough, it is not long before the first black-and-white striped face emerges from the sett: cautious at first, but with increasing confidence and eventually shuffling quickly over the compacted earth and away into the undergrowth on its nightly forage.

Badgers, our best-loved mammal, lead a secretive, timid existence, living in the overgrown and wild places of Wirral, their lives and abodes unseen and unknown by the majority of folk. Although by no means common, there are many more today than there were throughout most of the past hundred years. T. A. Coward stated in 1910 that 'In Wirral, if the badger now exists at all, it is rare'. Even in the mid-1800s the badger was so uncommon as to have its few known locations listed: at Hooton, Oxton and Caldy.

In 1934 a writer stated in a local magazine that he had 'definite proof' that badgers were back in Wirral in two separate localities, after an absence of forty years – the last having been shot in Burton in 1893.

The persecution of these lovely creatures is legendary; an old Wirral writer, Harry Neilson, recalls a small beer-shop run by one Micky O'Flynn, not far from Birkenhead Market in the 1870s. O'Flynn kept a badger in a barrel in a room at the back of the bar, and charged customers a fee for letting their dogs draw old 'Brock' from the barrel. Apparently the badger grew accustomed to the 'sport', and soon learned that it was less painful to come out quietly than to put up a fight with the dog. (O'Flynn eventually got apprehended for his cruelty when 'Brock' was seen scuffling along the gutter near the beer-house by a constable, who followed him home!)

The same writer recalls that badgers were plentiful in and around Bidston in the nineteenth century, the last one having been shot in 1892.

Today, they survive despite the odds being stacked against them. Secluded, hilly sites are rare in Wirral today, and in open, accessible country, they are easy prey for those people who seek 'sport' in digging them out to persecute and kill. Fortunately, we still have many large gardens in which badgers can live and breed in comparative safety, and these offer security for many families.

The badgers' living quarters, or setts, are dug in sloping ground, preferably where there is good cover such as gorse bushes, and often in woods or copses. A large sett – a network of tunnels and chambers – will have many entrances, and the size and scope of the sett is usually a good indication of the amount of activity in the badger community.

Their nocturnal activities out of the sett are usually in searching for food – earthworms, beetles and some fruits and vegetation – but also in playing and grooming.

It would be sad if these delightful creatures were to return to their former scarcity locally, and it is good to know that groups such as the Wirral & Cheshire Badger Group are vigilant and active in their concern for the present and future well-being of this fascinating mammal.

Red Rocks, Hoylake

The tip of Wirral, it is often called – the journey's end. From Chester, and all along the High Road, the signs all point to Hoylake. From here, the road goes no further. Next stop: Ireland, across 100 miles of Irish Sea. In the old days, when sailing-boats carried passengers from Wirral to Ireland, this was the last sight they had of Cheshire-land, this bright, wind-swept, rocky tip of Wirral.

This is river's-end too. This is where that great river, the Dee, after its long and often tortuous journey from Welsh highlands, through Cheshire lowlands, loses its identity and becomes one with the sea, a river no more.

This is a wonderful place, this wild land's-end of Wirral. I have known this place in all seasons, in all weathers, at all times of day and night. On golden summer afternoons when the dunes are bedecked with their colourful display of wild flowers, and butterflies dance from plant to plant. I have seen this exposed corner of Wirral ravaged by January gales sweeping in from the Irish Sea, the estuary a boiling grey cauldron of foam and spray. And I have walked along the beach on cold, clear, frosty January nights, the heavens a vault of blackness above the estuary, the stars of Orion dominating all, and the lights of buoys and light-vessels scarcely a glimmer across the endless, inky expanse of sea.

Jutting out into the estuary are the Red Stones, in ancient times the limit of the jurisdiction of the port of Chester. Stand on these rocks on a fine, clear summer's day, when the breeze blows in from the west, and take in the sky, the sea, the air – air which is probably the purest in England, having traversed miles of sea, moorland and mountain. Look southwards down the Dee, along the Wirral coastline. Westwards, towards the estuary, with the Hilbre Isles and, beyond, the hills of Wales. In the far distance, the Ormes of Llandudno, and perhaps a glimpse of Anglesey. Northwards, to the sea horizon, and occasionally the faint silhouette of Cumbrian and Scottish hills. And eastwards, along the north Wirral coast, to Lancashire and the Mersey, to lands of commerce and industry .

But these are all far away. Red Rocks itself has more than enough to offer, in its flowers, its birds, and its wildlife: beauty to complement the scenic backdrop beyond.

Burnet rose,
Red Rocks Marsh

Most of the land behind Red Rocks forms the Red Rocks Marsh Nature Reserve, managed by Cheshire Wildlife Trust, and one of their oldest reserves. It is a unique place, with an incredibly varied range of habitats: water-filled hollows, marshy ground, and reed-beds; wind-blown, sandy dunes facing the shore; dry, stable, grassy dunes along the edge of the golf course; and a few windswept bushes scattered about the place!

This place is constantly changing. Visit it one year, and when you come again twelve months later, it has changed. The gales which sweep in from the west and north-west mould and shape the reserve, scouring out new hollows, and blowing in sand from the estuary to fill former wet slacks. And wider changes are taking place on the estuary adjoining the marsh, where the former beach is rapidly becoming covered with grasses and plants.

How amazing then that such a volatile place can be so rich in life of all kinds – particularly the flowers. Over 200 different plants have been recorded in these ten acres: there are marsh-loving plants, such as orchids and iris; flowers of dry grassland – harebell, tormentil, and bedstraw; and plants which seem to thrive on barren, sandy places, such as the glorious sea holly. The burnet rose, pictured opposite, likes sandy places, and flowers not only here at Red Rocks, but also on other sites around the Wirral coast: on the Leasowe sand-dunes, above the Red Noses at New Brighton, and on the dunes at Meols. It is a spiny, prickly plant, which forms dense bushes by spreading its roots through the shallow sandy soil. Its hips are unusual too, in being a dark purply-black colour.

With such a glorious range of flowering plants, it is not surprising that this corner of Wirral should also boast a good population of butterflies and moths. Gatekeepers, graylings, meadow browns, wall browns, tortoiseshells, peacocks, common blues, skippers, and more, thrive in good summers, and add to the joys of a walk in and around the reserve.

Right: Meadow brown butterfly on thistle.

93

Sea holly on fore dunes, Red Rocks Marsh

The sun has shone from a cloudless sky since dawn, and the coastal dunes – the low, constantly shifting sandhills – have absorbed the day's heat. At times the gleaming sand has been hot to the touch, but now the sun is lowering over the estuary, and a pleasant coolness comes to the Wirral coast as a sea-breeze brings fresher air to our shores.

Few plants can survive such extremes of weather . . . changes in temperature, aridity, salty sea-spray, uprooting winds. But the sea holly not only survives, it thrives in such conditions. It is a beautiful and unusual plant, with its pale grey-green foliage, sharp, spikey leaves and metallic-blue flowers. The leaves have a thick outer skin which both prevents water loss and protects the plant from salty sea-spray.

In olden times, the roots of the sea holly were candied and sold as a delicacy called 'eringoes'. These were thought to have rejuvenating properties, and were mentioned by Falstaff in *The Merry Wives of Windsor*.

Grayling butterfly on sea holly, Red Rocks Marsh

Of all the butterflies we see in Wirral, this is one which is most likely to be found around the coast, particularly amongst the sand dunes. It will settle on plants or on stony ground, where it tilts its closed wings towards the sun, so as not to cast a shadow. This, together with its markings, helps to confuse predators. The grayling is not particularly rare, but it is local in its distribution.

Orchids, Red Rocks Marsh

One of the highlights of summer, for me and for many others, is the flowering of the orchids at Red Rocks Marsh. There are few grander sights anywhere in Wirral than this annual display of colour in such a lovely setting.

The range of colours of these hybrid orchids is quite amazing, ranging from almost-white right through to the darkest purple, with all shades in between. There are big ones and small ones, tall ones and short ones. They seem to thrive in the rather damp, perhaps slightly saline wet area at the northern end, a site which was not mentioned a hundred years ago in a survey of Wirral plants. The same survey did, however, state that marsh orchids were found in the Wallasey sandhills and in meadows between Leasowe and Meols.

These orchids have good years and bad years. Just when one is pessimistically thinking that they are disappearing from Red Rocks, the following summer they bloom in all their abundant glory. Let us hope that these lovely plants survive the radical changes taking place around the estuary.

Five-spot burnet moth on orchid, Red Rocks Marsh

These attractive moths are abundant in this marshy area, where its caterpillars feed on bird's-foot trefoil.

The insects, with their striking red spots on an irridescent greenish-black background, are great survivors, as they are extremely poisonous to predators. Their bodies contain derivatives of cyanide, formed by the caterpillars through the food-plants, which are eventually passed on to the grown moth.

This adult moth is seen resting on the flower-spike of an orchid.

Harebell, Red Noses, New Brighton

New Brighton means different things to different people: to some, it is a place in which to enjoy an invigorating stroll along the parade; to others it is a place from which to fish; others enjoy the entertainments. One of its best places though, for me, is the fine, grassy ridge of the old cliff-line which starts at the Red Noses and continues for half-a-mile to Harrison Drive.

Here is a world far removed from the amusement palaces and bingo halls. This, one thinks, is how the Wallasey coast must have looked before man came along and tamed it: craggy sandstone outcrops, with patches of flower-decked turf and gorse bushes. The sea laps the cliffs no more, alas – but it is not far away, over the promenade wall, and its smell, its sound, are ever present on these heights.

Right: Summer sunset over Red Rocks Marsh

Grey seals, Dee Estuary

One of the great joys of tramping across the sands of the Dee Estuary for a spell on Hilbre is the prospect of seeing the seals – as a group from a distance, or perhaps one or two individuals at closer quarters.

One's first awareness is usually of an eery moaning sound coming from the direction of Wales, often heard well before reaching the middle isle, if the wind is right. Once over the bar, the colony is obvious – a smudge of grey on the sandbank opposite. Through the binoculars, the smudge becomes a large group of individuals – perhaps as many as 200 – lounging around on the bank by the water's edge.

Can this be the same part of Britain in which, only eighty years ago, the visit of a grey seal to these waters was a rare enough occasion to warrant the event being recorded in naturalists' notebooks: '. . . seals have on at least three occasions visited Cheshire waters. On October 28th 1909 a young grey seal was stranded on a bank off Hoylake and captured by some fishermen and . . . exhibited to the public'?

The seals first began to be seen regularly about sixty years ago, and numbers have maintained a level at about 200, with small fluctuations from year to year. It is thought that the Dee seals originated from a large colony at Ramsey island, in west Wales, and have found

conditions on the West Hoyle Bank to their liking, presumably because there is a plentiful supply of food in the estuary.

But whatever their origins, or their reasons for being here, their presence is an added bonus to a day out in the estuary: what could be more thrilling than to see these strange mammals swimming around Hilbre, at times coming quite close to the shore, and looking at us as inquisitively as we look at them!

Midsummer sunset, Dee Estuary

The Dee Estuary is Wirral's most precious asset. It is a place of beauty, of peace and tranquility, a place of wide open spaces where it is possible to leave behind, for a while, our land-based cares and enjoy the smells, the sights and the sounds of a truly wild place.

There are many folk, of course, who care little for the birds, the plants, the mammals, but still love the sunsets, the peace of the estuary; people who simply enjoy an occasional walk around the marine lake, perhaps, or a stroll along the boardwalk at Red Rocks. How lovely to see, on a summer's evening, so many taking the opportunity to experience, perhaps after a trying day at work, the natural things, the beautiful things, which are on our doorstep: summer joys are fleeting, and the season passes all too quickly.

A local naturalist summed up this place seventy years ago:

'How can I envisage in words that insistent call that comes to some of us, the call of the running tide, the longing to set foot once again on the saltings, to smell the tang of the sea air, to hear the sound of rubber boots squelching over soft mud, or the sleepy murmur of ocean rollers breaking on a distant sandbank. . . . Those of us who have heard the wild call of the running tide must go down to the sea again and again to watch the passing pageant of migration . . . in summer heat or winter cold, the estuary still draws us to its shingle beaches, its saltings, or its freezing mudflats, to watch the bird life of the foreshore . . .'

Intake Wood, Raby Mere

Autumn

AUTUMN is not so much a season as a feeling, an inner experience of transition from lightness to darkness, from warmth to cold, from life to death, from growth to decay. It is seen outwardly well enough, in the yellowing of the leaves, the dying of the grasses and plants, in nature's preparing for the long dark months ahead. But it is also felt deep inside our beings: that soft, almost melancholy resignation that, just as we cannot fight the march of time in our lives, so the passing of the year is inevitable. The drawing-in of the evenings, the chill in the air, the seasonal mists, the early frosts, all tell us that the year's peak is past, and the downhill slide to mid-winter has begun.

Some years one feels a hint of autumn as early as August, particularly during droughty summers which cause the leaves to start yellowing and falling early, when the blackberries ripen ahead of their due season, and when the hedgerows seem a dusty yellow after weeks of warm, dry, anticyclonic weather.

Yet in other years, perhaps more typical of our damp, westerly climate, the abundant rains of summer keep the foliage green until mid-October, and only the prolific fungi of our woods remind us that the year is well advanced; when a sudden, sharp frost causes the trees to turn almost overnight. Then the Wirral landscape turns

Velvet shank fungus, Thornton Wood, Raby Mere

golden-bronze for a short spell until the gales of the next Atlantic depression tear the foliage from the trees, bringing another sudden change, to winter, with little of autumn in between.

For some, this season is the best of the year: they love the colours, the smells, the soft quality of light, the slowing down of life after the liveliness of spring and summer; and they enjoy the prospect of dark evenings by the fire, relaxing with a book after the day's chores are over.

Others though see the season differently: they see the end of the freedom

and light of the long warm, sunny days of summer; they see autumn as the beginning of the gloom and chill of the year's dark period, and eagerly await the passing of the solstice, when the sun begins to rise a little earlier each day, bringing the promise of spring to their hearts once again.

I see autumn in Wirral as a series of cameos, small scenes from local life that epitomise the season for me and, no doubt, for many other Wirral folk too. Foremost are the colourful images of our trees: from the majestic woodland oaks and beeches of Eastham, Dibbinsdale and Storeton to the softer birches of Bidston, Thurstaston and Heswall. We are suddenly aware of trees that we have hardly noticed through the rest of the year – in our towns and villages, lining our roads and highways, and in suburban and country gardens. Beneath the trees I see children – and adults too – in red wellies, enjoying kicking through the deep leaf-litter, searching for shiny conkers.

I see misty November mornings on the high heaths of Wirral, the damp, decaying vegetation white with spiders' webs, with just a few bedraggled rabbits scurrying through the undergrowth.

Wirral autumns sometimes have golden October days, with weather borrowed from

Right: October sunshine captures the colours of a beech tree in Thornton Wood Nature Reserve, Dibbinsdale

summer – blue skies and a gentle breeze from the south-west – when I tramp across the shining sands of the Dee Estuary, Hilbre-bound. Such days are good for birds, and I see clouds of knot and dunlin performing acrobats above the mudflats, their shrieks filling the air with sound.

On other October days of a different kind, I see the north Wirral coast being lashed by equinoctial gales blowing the Irish Sea high above the embankments of Moreton and the promenades of New Brighton, Meols and Hoylake. On such days these wild winds sweeping in from the west will shred the leaves from exposed trees, leaving little autumnal colour for the remainder of the season.

Autumnal cameos include September Sunday afternoons in Royden Park, with families enjoying a last taste of summer, as they and their children romp through the rhododendron bushes, or sit quietly in the walled garden soaking up the still-warm sunshine.

I see too the pleasant village streets of Burton and Shotwick in mid-autumn, with the last of the summer flowers still decorating the front gardens of the old cottages which make up these lovely, ancient, and typically Cheshire villages. Or low evening sunlight catching the whitewashed quayside buildings of Parkgate, the reed-beds silhouetted against the glowing, fiery sky.

These, and many more, are the autumn images which I know and love. They are to be enjoyed, savoured: for the season is short, and beyond lie the long, dark winter months . . . but even in this season of apparent decay, one does not have to look far to see the signs of new life, of nature's rebirth to come, in the tightly enclosed buds on oak and ash trees: spring in autumn.

Left: Orb-web spider

Right: a misty day on Thurstaston Common

Royden Park, Frankby

The mixed woodlands which fringe Royden Park blend with the birch woods of Thurstaston Common's heathland to form a glorious, varied landscape within a very small area. Lovely at any time of the year, they are particularly attractive in October as the leaves yellow and fall to the many pathways, forming golden trails through the undergrowth.

Birds such as the blue tit *(right)* are a common sight in such woods, and colourful fungi emerge in response to the warm, gentle rains of the season.

Royden Park, Frankby

Seasonal mists rise from the mudflats of the Dee and enshroud the woodlands which cover these high lands above the estuary. Already the trees have lost their autumnal colours, their leaves shaken and scattered by the first gales of the season blowing in from the Atlantic.

The deep leaf-litter of this and previous autumns will gradually settle to provide a rich and fertile humus in which tree seedlings will grow and develop into new woodlands for our future enjoyment.

Left: Brick-cap fungus, Thurstaston Common

Dibbinsdale

The wooded river-valleys of Dibbinsdale wear a rich raiment of colour at this time of the year. The flowers of spring are but a distant memory, and the riverbanks and steep valley sides are now covered with a thick carpet of decaying oak, beech and sycamore leaves.

Autumn seems to linger here in these east-Wirral woods, which suffer less from the seasonal gales than the woodlands on the western side of the peninsula. When the branches are bare on the trees of Bidston, Caldy and Heswall, the oaks and beeches of these ancient, sheltered woods are aglow with warm colour.

Pleurotus cornucopiae, Stapledon Wood, Caldy

The ancient woods of Wirral are rich in fungi, many of which grow on fallen or rotting timber. This edible fungus is often found on stumps of our native deciduous trees such as elm or oak, where it forms dense, creamy-coloured fan-like clusters.

Caldy Hill

The high sandstone ridges of west Wirral are clothed in golden yellow during October with the coming of the colder days of autumn. The birch woods of Caldy Hill, Thurstaston Common and Heswall Dales are comparative newcomers to the landscape of these Deeside hills, for old photos show long stretches of bare, craggy heathland as far as the eye can see.

Sheep grazing probably kept the silver birches from spreading in the past, but today much of our former heathland has been smothered by these intrusive but beautiful trees. And lovely they are, in spring when their gossamer green leaves are bursting from their buds; in autumn, when their leaves glow in the mellow October sunlight; and in winter, when the delicate tracery of their twigs and branches shows clear against the sharp blue sky.

One of my favourite places in Wirral is a quiet clearing in the birch woods on Caldy Hill, where on a warm autumn afternoon one can perch on the craggy sandstone outcrops and see through the trees the wide expanse of the estuary, its wet sands glistening under a cloudless sky: autumnal magic!

Fly agaric, birch woods

One of the joys of walking through Wirral's birch woods in autumn is to see the reappearance of this, one of our most colourful and easily recognised fungi.

Seen in its early stages as a small red-and-white spotted ball, it soon grows into a huge, dinner-plate size plant conspicuous amongst the yellowing bracken beneath the silver birches.

Its poisonous and intoxicating properties were well recognised by medieval folk, who broke the plant's flesh into bowls of milk which were then used to stupefy flies; hence its name.

Autumn mists, Thurstaston Common

By late autumn, Wirral's heathlands – on Caldy, Thurstaston and Bidston Hills, and Heswall Dales – are looking decidedly wintry. The heather is well and truly finished, the bracken has died back to a rich russet brown, and the birches are shedding the last of their bronzing leaves.

Yet these lovely heathlands have a certain magic of their own at this season, especially when the dank morning mists swirl about the crags and copses – 'an Exmoor in miniature' as one local writer described them many years ago.

On such mornings these small heaths can feel like vast moors: there is an eerie silence, save for the occasional cry of a jay or a passing curlew, or the yaffle of a green woodpecker from a nearby copse.

With gossamer-like spiders' webs, drenched with dew, covering the gorse bushes and heather patches, this is a different world, a place to be left alone to wild nature, where it seems a sacrilege for the human foot to venture

Hedgerow fruits, near Thornton Hough

Some of my earliest recollections are of blackberrying as a child: expeditions were not necessary, for our hedgerowed countryside began at our front door, and an afternoon's collecting would net 10 to 15 pounds of fruit, all gathered within hailing distance of home.

What a contrast are these autumnal hedgerows to the fresh green growth and fragile flowers of spring – a wild tangle of bronzing leaves, rich red berries and purple fruit, laced with dew-heavy webs and upturned nests.

Myths, legends and superstitions surround our bramble-bushes. Poorly children were passed through a bramble-arch, rooted at each end, to make them well again, and this procedure was also believed to cure rheumatism.

An ancient story recounts how satan, as he was being cast out of Paradise, fell into a bramble bush and cursed it roundly. He is said to spit or urinate on the plant on each anniversary of the Fall, hence the superstition that one should not pick blackberries after old St Michaelmas Day, 11th October, as the berries will be sour!

Left: Hawthorn berries add a splash of colour to a hedge near Heswall

Rose hips,
hedgerow near Raby Mere

It seems only a short time ago that the hedgerows of high summer were laden with flower-blossoms: wild rose, elder and may. This succession of flowering colour has given way to the fulfilment of autumn, and the roses, the elders and the hawthorns are now bearing their seasonal fruits.

Winemakers relish the season, with its abundant produce for the taking, but in times past country folk took the best fruits from the hedgerows for preserving throughout the long, lean winter months.

Rose hips have long been used as a rich source of vitamins, and countless generations of children have been brought up on the benefits of rose-hip syrup.

Robin,
Stapledon Wood, Caldy

The fruits and berries which ripen on the hedgerows throughout autumn provide a constant source of food for many of our birds. The hedge will also provide roosting sites and shelter from the seasonal winds and rains.

The robin is mainly insectivorous but will also eat fruit and seeds in season. One of our best-loved garden birds, the robin is also to be found in woodland areas and hedges. The bird is resident in this country throughout the year; whilst the male and female have similar plumage the young birds are speckled brown and do not develop the familiar red breast until their first autumn.

The Dee marshes, near Parkgate

The marshes in autumn are rather sad-looking: the late summer splash of colour offered by the sea aster is over, and the marsh grasses and reeds are yellowing and dying. Yet the season brings much to enjoy out on these wide-reaching acres of pools, gutters and marsh-banks: autumn skies often bring the best light effects to the estuary, with lengthening shadows and equinoctial cloud-patterns painting a landscape rich in tone and colour.

Although the seasonal gathering of the wader-flocks is best seen down-river, towards the mouth of the estuary, the acrobatics of the wader-flocks are still a spectacular sight when viewed from the Dee marshlands, and many bird-watchers gather along the Wirral coastline at times of exceptional high tides to see the birds flushed from their feeding grounds into the sky.

The magic of the Dee marshes has lured many folk to explore their vast reaches, in search of the birds to capture with a gun or on film. One such was Guy Farrar, a local naturalist of the early years of this century, who came to his love of birds one autumn day on the estuary:

'Once, many years ago, when, as a boy, I was out on the saltings after geese, I saw a fleeting glimpse of the beauty of bird life, a momentary picture of breathtaking loveliness that turned me for ever into a bird watcher and a lover of birds. It was a dull November day, a leaden sky and a chill north wind giving a promise of coming snow. I was tramping across the saltings, when suddenly from out of the grey-green marsh grass there arose a cloud of what appeared to be snowflakes, hovering and dancing in the winter air.

'I stood entranced! I had never before seen snow buntings, and here, at my feet, were these tiny pilgrims from the north performing their fairy ballet for my own special edification. The dance of the snowflakes lasted but a few moments; with shrill twitterings the whole flock floated earthwards, alighting amongst some dead stems of sea aster. The vision faded but, at that moment, a new and enthusiastic bird-watcher was born.'

A hundred thousand birds on the Dee Estuary

Autumn's pageant of colour ashore, in the trees, woods and hedgerows, is equalled by a spectacle offshore which is just as glorious: the annual gathering of wader-birds on their migration from the rapidly cooling northern latitudes to the warmer climes of the south.

People come from all over Wirral, and beyond, to experience the thrill of the aerobatic displays of massed clouds of knot and dunlin sweeping over the glistening sands and mud-flats of our coastline. All around our coast, from the rocky shoreline at Eastham, up the banks of the Mersey to the estuary at New Brighton, then along the North Wirral coast with its wide, open sands; to the mud-flats of the Dee Estuary, a rich feeding-ground for tired waders. Each stretch has its attractions for the birds, and although many folk say they are fewer in number than they used to be, this seasonal display still has an awesome magic, a power to thrill.

Seventy-five years ago, a local naturalist described the spectacle:

'Wet sands, crossed here and there by shallow gutters, stretched seaward and across the wide Dee Estuary as far as the eye could reach; the Welsh shore, five miles distant, was hidden in thick mist. Nearly a mile from the land runs a long sandstone ridge or reef, which at high tide splits into the three islets of Hilbre; the smallest and most southerly, the Eye, was our destination, as three hours before full flow we splashed bare-foot through the remnants of the last tide.

Gulls were drifting up the main, but the tide had not yet begun to fill the gutters, which are seldom if ever empty before the next inflow refills them. Away seaward a line of foam marked the advancing waters, breaking over the East Hoyle; the red and black buoys in Hilbre Swash heeled landward; the big tide was coming, but there was still time to cross comfortably from the mainland.

Then between the two larger islands the lapping water crept in swift trickles, first filling the ripple marks, then swamping them altogether. Bare-footed cocklers trudged back towards West Kirby, and two belated visitors to the main island raced knee-deep through the swelling strait which now separated the two. We were left in sole possession of our observatory, a few square yards of turf clinging to the rocky outcrop, wave-washed in storm, windswept at all times, but a great gathering place for birds.

When from Hilbre to the Red Rocks was one unbroken sheet of water, and the gutter which cut us off from the land a rushing torrent, our sport began. We peeped over the bank, levelling glasses on the noisy crowd which lined the ever-swelling Swash. Middle Hilbre was alive with birds; they crowded, black masses over its lower rocks, whilst herring, common, and black-headed gulls flitted uneasily over the racing waters.

A twittering flock of linnets danced in the air round the Eye for a few minutes, then made for the Cheshire shore; but two land-birds, a young wheatear and a song thrush, were on the island when we arrived, and we left them there; they were reluctant to leave their island oasis. Both, doubtless, had selected it as a resting place on their southward journey.

No word-picture can adequately describe the thrilling music of the sandbanks: the curlew's wild, clear call; the triple note of the whimbrel; the sharp bark of the godwit; the liquid whistle of the grey plover; the purr of the dunlin; and the noisy yelp of the redshank were mingled

continually with the music of the sea-pies. Hour after hour the sound swelled or died down, but the birds were never silent.

The first waders which sought the still uncovered rocks which fringe the grass-grown portion of the Eye were dunlin and ringed plovers; they arrived in flocks of from a score to several hundred birds, wheeled around, flashing silvery white as they all turned their underparts towards us, swept past with a rustle as of many silken skirts, then settled almost at our feet. Some tucked their bills into their scapulars, raised one leg, and dozed; others attended to their plumage but, whether awake or, apparently, asleep, they hopped nearer and nearer as the water pushed them up the sloping rocks.

Then came a lull. The last bank of empty cockle shells was covered in the little muddy inlets, cut deep in the blue clay; the last sea-pie deserted the rocks at our feet. It was past high tide, and the birds had moved to make the most of the ebb; the only avian companion left, beside the wheatear and thrush, was a lively fly-catching rock pipit, who absolutely ignored our presence.

When the gutter was again fordable, a huge expanse of sand stretched once more towards the Welsh shore, and to the anchored fishing-boats, now heeled over, in the gutter off the stranded port of Parkgate.'

Curlew, off Hilbre

There can be few autumnal sounds more expressive of the sadness of the season than the lonely call of the curlew in the late afternoon of a November day. Whether winging its solitary way across the wet sands of the Dee Estuary, or flying high above mid-Wirral fields, the call of this enigmatic bird captures the essence of autumn.

When curlews return to the estuary and the coasts of Wirral, I know that winter is not far away, for these birds which breed in spring up in the moorlands of Wales return to our shores for the winter season. Here they will forage for cockles on the edge of the receding tide, until the call of a new spring beckons them again to their breeding-grounds beyond the Dee.

Winter

Snow covers the woodland floor at Stapledon Wood, Caldy

FOOTPRINTS in the snow; hoar-frost on leaf-litter; icicles draped on Dungeon waterfall; storm-lashed cliffs and promenades; January snowdrops in Shotwick Dell: these are some of my images of Wirral's natural places in a typical winter.

But is there such a thing as a typical Wirral winter? Some years – perhaps most – we experience little or no snow, and that which does fall lies but briefly. Usually, the season is mild and damp, with wet and windy weather systems marching towards us from the Atlantic to drench our woods and meadows. Such periods give us superb skies, raging sunsets, and restless landscapes.

Christmas-card scenes are rare, but some winters give us occasional spells of cold, continental weather, with long nights of hard frosts which kill off the still-flowering gorse on Caldy Hill and the remnants of campion surviving in sheltered hedge-banks and field-corners. During such spells the marsh-pools of the Dee estuary freeze over, and the herons and other birds of these wild places fight for survival.

Some Wirral places have a magic all of their own during the winter months. I think of the silent wooded vaults of the ancient river-valleys which radiate from Raby Mere like spokes of a wheel: giant

Above: A typical winter-garden scene in suburban Wirral: a robin perches on snow-covered ivy – a splash of colour amidst the season's drab tints

Right: the attractive cladonia lichen gives a rare splash of colour on mossy ground on heathland during the winter months

Far right: winter frosts clothe the remnants of bracken and heather on Thurstaston Hill

oaks and ash trees which were formless in their summer raiment now stand stark against the cold sky, each an individual with a unique character of shapely trunk and branches reaching up to the light.

These same woodlands will, in high summer, be impenetrable – a tangled mass of undergrowth and luxuriant vegetation fighting for what little light penetrates the foliage of the trees overhead. But throughout the winter months they are light and airy, the cleansing wind of the season swirling through the tree-tops high above the damp valley-floor.

I see too the beauty of our high, heathy places at the turn of the year: frost-shrouded bracken fronds, dead but still standing proud; and damp hollows fringed with silver birch trees, silent and still save for the occasional cry of jay or magpie.

But what of our coastal areas in winter? What does the season bring to our estuaries, sea-coast, mudflats and islands? Here indeed is a changed scene: gone are the wild flowers of summer, the sun-scorched turf and the warm sands. Only the birds remain, the waders who find here a safe haven, a feeding and resting ground through the dark months until springtime calls them to head north again.

Left: Rare winter's snow blankets the trees on Thurstaston Hill

Above: Oyster-catchers bring a splash of colour to the Dee estuary on a fine day in December

The coastal landscape of Wirral is at its best in these volatile days of stormy skies and heavy seas: when a 32-foot swell runs past the jetty at Eastham, or a force 9 gale lashes the waves of the Irish Sea against the Black Rock at New Brighton; when the seas around the Red Rocks are boiling, white, turbulent, and the isles of Hilbre are hidden in a fog of wind-blown sea-spray.

And, after the storms have passed, clear blue skies return to Wirral: the coastal waters become calm again, the noisy seas abate. For a while all is at peace.

Inland, the woods and heathlands become quiet, the trees motionless. As night approaches, a hard frost forms on twigs and branches; whilst above, the black, cloudless sky is bespeckled with stars and planets. This is Wirral in winter.

Woodland, Arrowe Country Park

For twelve years of my life I lived within a stone's-throw of Arrowe Park, and during that time got to know its wild corners well, particularly the fine woods which clothe its edges and form lovely stands by the lake. John Ralph Shaw, who planted the fine woodlands back in the mid-1800s, was surely a man of vision: but I wonder if even he could have foreseen how his tiny saplings would one day mature into the beautiful woods we see today.

Nicholson's plantation, Neilson's plantation, Card plantation: nondescript names for wild woods which in springtime are rich in campion, stitchwort, violets, ferns and primroses; but even in winter have a special beauty all of their own. Here, in the depths of the season, on those days when frosts keep the leaves white from dawn to dusk, holly bushes and honeysuckles still bear bright berries for birds and squirrels. Fallen trees, uprooted by storms of earlier winters and rotting into the ground-vegetation, are green with mosses and lichens. And, amidst these decaying remnants, there will appear traces of new life: the swelling bud of an oak seedling perhaps, emerging from the deadness of winter: a harbinger of spring.

Blackbird, suburban garden, Caldy

Although long, snowy spells are rare in this part of the world, such conditions do cause problems for many of our popular songbirds. At times like this, many birds forsake their usual haunts and habitats and try their luck in the gardens of our homes. These birds rely on the thoughtfulness and generosity of folk who put out bread, fat and other morsels; without such help, many of our favourite songbirds would perish and our gardens and beauty spots would be all the poorer without these common but popular creatures.

Winter snow, Stapledon Wood, Caldy Hill

To those who know and enjoy the beauty of the woodlands which clothe Caldy Hill – beech, oak and ash on the lower, south-facing slopes and birch trees on the upper reaches – in spring, summer and autumn, with all the richness that those seasons give, the starkness of the place under winter's snow comes as a surprise.

The woodland floor, in winter still a tangle of brambles, ivy, dead bracken and fern fronds, is a flat mantle of white, the usual undulations of peat and rock made level by this soft layer of snow. It is a magical, haunting place: a vault of white silence, broken only by the occasional call of jay or magpie echoing through the trees, or the soft sighing of the wind through the highest branches.

On days like this, the woods of Wirral lose their individuality, their uniqueness: the blanket of snow makes the woods of Eastham, Storeton, Burton, Arrowe, Bidston, as one. On such days, only the distant glimpse of snow-shrouded landscapes, with their familiar landmarks, offers visual clues: enjoy them, for they are rare enough in Wirral winters.

Long-tailed tit and blue tit, wooded garden

Although we usually associate blue tits with our suburban gardens nowadays, they are really most at home in and around woods. What an active life they seem to lead, never for once stopping to just sit and sing! Their life seems to be one non-stop round of feverish activity: it has been observed that blue tits can make as many as one hundred forays an hour from the nest for food at the height of the breeding season!

Wirral is ideal territory for both the long-tailed tit (left) and the blue tit, with plenty of woodland-type areas of the natural kind and of the garden variety. In the winter months, long-tailed tits move through the woodlands and hedgerows in small parties, always on the move in search of food. They occasionally visit bird-tables when they will all descend at once for a few minutes before moving on.

Sadly, severe winters can decimate the long-tailed tit population, although numbers recover quickly – usually eight to twelve eggs are laid in their beautiful domed nests made of moss and lichen, held together with hair and cobwebs and lined with hundreds of feathers.

Thurstaston Hill

Can this be the same place that, only six months ago, was aglow with the warm purple bloom of heather and the rich yellow fire of gorse? Where families picnicked on the soft, warm turf and a mild, sweet breeze blew in from the Welsh hills?

Today, after days of keen winds blowing in from the east, these high lands above the Dee are in the grip of winter's worst: they took the brunt of the snow showers which swept across Wirral overnight, and sub-zero temperatures have frozen solid the few pools scattered about this high heath.

It is a hard time for the few animals and birds that usually live in and around these Wirral moors: those animals that have not hibernated – the fox in particular – will seek food and even shelter in the suburbs; but the woodpeckers and jays will have a difficult time finding food on these ice-bound heaths. They will eke out a meagre existence for the hopefully short duration of these Arctic-like conditions, until the mild, sweet westerly wind once again brings life and warmth to these high places of Wirral.

Hoar-frost on gorse, Heswall Dales

'When the gorse is in flower, then kissing is in fashion' – so runs an old rhyme; another states that 'While the gorse is in flower, Britain will never be conquered'. The bright splash of yellow lights up even the most dreary days of winter and, whilst the flowers will no doubt die after being touched by the hoar-frost, new buds will come along to open up on the next spell of mild winter weather.

Such a common local plant has inevitably been used by Wirral folk down the ages: villagers used to clean out their chimneys by dropping down the flues a bunch of gorse with a stone attached. In the windy parts of the peninsula women-folk use to lay out their washing to dry upon gorse-bushes, the sharp spikes preventing the clothes from being blown away.

In some winters, the green shoots of the gorse are the only succulent morsels to be found on our heaths, and many animals will resort to eating the sharp, spiked stems for nourishment.

Thor's Stone, Thurstaston Hill

The moon rises over the rocky crags of Thor's Stone on a January evening: the bright glow in the sky at this hour of the day signifies that the longest night is past, and that the evenings are, ever so slowly but surely, pulling out again.

With clearing skies a frosty night is in store, a frost that will clothe the rushes and reeds in the nearby pools with a dusty whiteness: otherwise ordinary shapes will take on a new beauty, a cold starkness against the dark, icy waters.

The old stones of Thurstaston and the other uplands of Wirral – Bidston, Storeton, Heswall and West Kirby – have been trodden and used by all generations down the ages: for work, for play, in toil and in leisure. These old rocks lie scattered about these high places, worn by time, the wind and the rain. None, however, can have been so greatly worn as this slab of blood-red stone in its stately amphitheatre: worn by the feet of thousands of youngsters eager to reach its summit, to attain the peak of peaks in this place of winter beauty.

146

Reedmace and ladybird, Royden Park

Park? What a misnomer! Here you will find no flower-beds, or swings, or neatly trimmed lawns: more a wild, natural extension of Thurstaston Common, with grassy meadows, woods and ponds. It is at its best in spring and summer, but even in the depths of winter there is beauty – and life – particularly in and around the meres and ponds.

Many folk call these frost-shrouded plants bulrushes, but their correct title is reedmace. They grow in most wet places in Wirral, and are at their best in mid-winter, before the birds and weather rip their majestic seed-heads to shreds.

In times past, their fluffy seed-heads were used to stuff pillows and mattresses, and their strong, waxy leaves were used for basket-weaving. Now there seems to be another use for these beautiful plants: as a home for a sheltering ladybird!

Frozen pools, Burton Marsh

It was one of those quiet, overcast, cold, grey days early in the new year: the Wirral landscape, in every direction, was featureless. There was no colour: no greenery, even, for a sharp overnight frost had failed to thaw during the day, despite a little watery sunlight. Down by the marshes, from the footpath to Burton Point, the Welsh hills were just discernible through the cold haze; otherwise, the only points of interest were the few bedraggled-looking sheep grazing on what shoots of grass survived.

If we had stayed on the path, the day would have been dull, uninteresting, featureless. However, stepping out onto the frozen marshland, another world presented itself: a myriad of pools, frozen across with concentric patterns formed in the ice. Hundreds of them, reflecting and scattering the weak daylight at random angles and in all directions, as far as the eye could see. An unpromising day had turned into a magical experience.

Opposite: Winter skies at Red Rocks Marsh, Hoylake

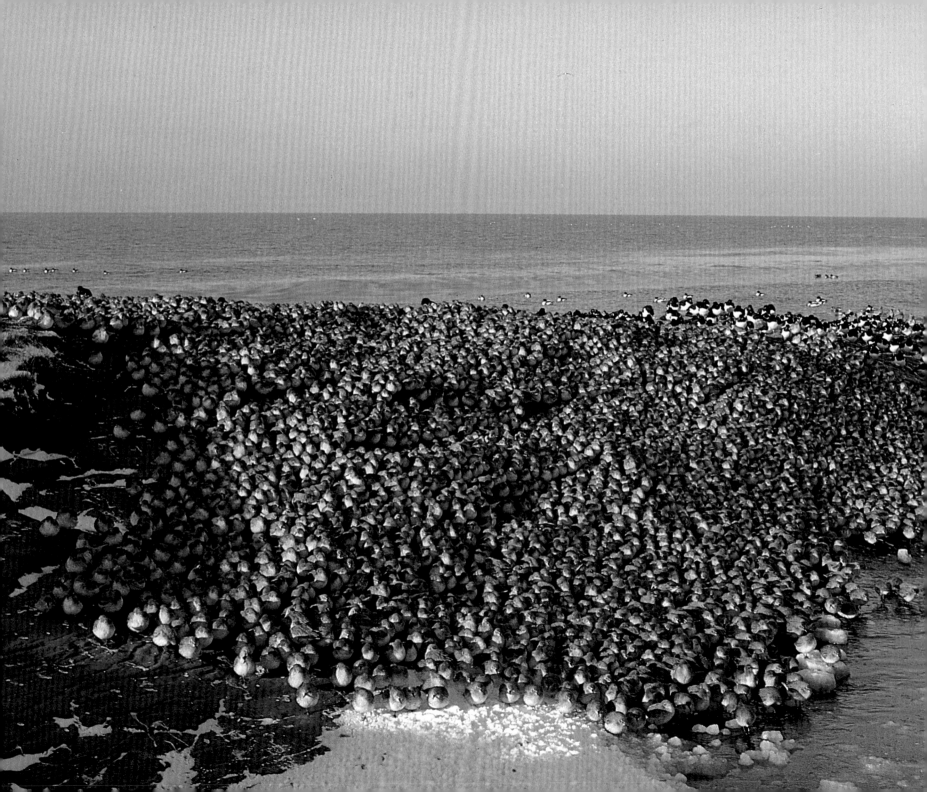

Wader flocks at rest and in flight, Hilbre

One of the great things about the succession of mid-winter depressions that march from west to east across our country, is that there is usually a fine, but brief, spell of bright, settled weather in between each weather-system. Such spells bring blue skies, calm atmosphere, and bright sunlight shining from low in the sky.

On the rising tide waders cease to feed and mass themselves tightly together on the few acres left uncovered. This flock of several thousand knot is accompanied by a few oyster-catchers and curlew, with shelduck to be seen on the water.

After resting awhile on the rocky edges of Hilbre, the birds get increasingly restless and, aware that the tide is receding, there comes a point at which, as if with one accord and with one mind, they decide to take to the air and leave their rocky haven for the foodstocks of the mudflats.

Knot and oyster-catcher, Little Eye

Considerable numbers of both knot and oyster-catcher, and some other waders, remain as winter residents, and they can be seen all around the Wirral coastline, from Stanlow Point right round to the upper Dee marshes, when tidal and weather conditions are favourable.

Curlew and oyster-catcher, Dee Estuary

There can be few sounds more haunting than the cry of the curlew as it flies across the vast expanse of wet mud-flats. It is an evocative sound, bringing to mind other landscapes, far removed from our coastal regions: of far-distant moorlands and fellsides. Many's the night I have stood in my garden, in the darkness of the midnight hour, and heard flocks of curlews calling as they flew overhead; passing mysteriously from where to where I do not know, but disappearing into the distance like ghosts in the dark.

Wader-flocks at sunset, Dee Estuary

Mid-winter: a calm, settled day has brought a fine sunset across the Dee Estuary. The Welsh hills are clothed in a misty haze, and flocks of birds settle on the wet sands. Cloudless skies will bring an air-frost to these parts, and a ground-frost to the marshes higher up the estuary. One who loved Wirral's bird-life, Guy Farrar, wrote these words about winter around Wirral's coasts sixty years ago:

'For a picture of utter desolation, it would be hard to find a better setting than saltings in a hard frost. Bird life has vanished from its usual haunts – the feathered folk of the estuary, the ducks and waders, are hard put to find the means of existence. For a few brief hours, day and night, the mudflats are thawed by the ebb and flow of the tide, and only during that short space is food available. Then comes the thaw, and once more the saltings wake to life. In the half light of a winter's evening the whee-ous of widgeon can be heard returning to their flashes, and the grey geese flight to and from their inland feeding grounds at dawn and dusk. The memory of hard times fades, the life of the estuary resumes its normal cycle, a cycle governed entirely by the ebb and flow of the tides.'

About the photography

The photographs in this book are the result of hundreds of hours spent in the Wirral countryside over many years observing and photographing its wildlife and habitats.

In order to convey the true feeling of the countryside the photographer has to become familiar with the natural world, to spend time in the field, and to patiently observe the landscape and its wildlife in all weathers and seasons.

An appreciation of the effect of light is essential; it is, after all, simply light falling on a piece of film which creates a photographic image. Light is far more atmospheric early on a misty morning than when the sun is overhead at mid-day; a subject back-lit may have more impact than if seen in flat frontal lighting; diffused sun will soften harsh shadows – the choice of lighting can make the difference between the success or failure of a photograph.

Sometimes it is necessary to use flash, for example when photographing mammals at night, or capturing small birds in flight but, even then, lighting has to be carefully balanced to simulate, as far as possible, the effects of natural light, be it sunlight or moonlight.

Always mindful of the foregoing, the nature photographer will nevertheless wish to acquire a fair amount of equipment to tackle the challenges of the natural world, be it photographing a wading bird with a powerful telephoto lens, a delicate orchid in close-up, or an autumn woodland scene. For those interested in the technicalities I give more details below, but the most important consideration is rugged, reliable equipment with good-quality lenses.

Equipment

Camera bodies: Nikon FE2 and 801S. Lenses: Nikkor 24mm, 55mm, 105mm micro, 70–210 zoom (Tamron), 300mm and 500mm IFED.

For certain applications I use a Bronica ETRSi medium format camera giving transparencies of 6 x 4.5cm.

Lenses: 40mm, 75mm, 100mm macro and 200mm. This camera system is used when possible for landscapes and in other circumstances where powerful telephoto lenses are not necessary.

One special piece of equipment I use is a high-speed flash unit powering four heads which discharge with a flash duration of only 1/20,000th of a second. If the subject is lit wholly by flash it follows that only the brief instant of the flash discharge is registered on the film and thus extremely rapid movements can be 'frozen'. The flash unit is used in conjunction with an infra-red beam and triggering unit to fire the camera at the precise instant that the subject is in the frame and, hopefully, in focus. The Bronica system is used for high-speed flash work. For more static subjects simple conventional flash-guns are used.

So far as I can recall, all the photographs in this book were taken with the aid of a tripod or, in a few cases, a monopod.

Film

Over the years I have used a variety of films, and improved emulsions are coming onto the market all the time. Certain films can be more suitable than others under different lighting conditions. Recently, I have been using Ektachrome Elite 100 for

Swallows nesting on a beam in a converted barn in Caldy

35mm work and Fujichrome Provia (100 ASA) and Fujichrome Velvia (50 ASA) for medium format.

Filters

None of the photographs in this book have had the colours enhanced. The only filters I use are: an 81B warm-up filter occasionally for times when the lighting is excessively blue, for example during the middle of the day, in order to bring the colours back to a more natural rendering; a neutral grey graduated filter to balance the brightness of the sky with the foreground on landscape photographs; and a polarising filter to cut reflections on water, to help improve haze penetration and to make clouds stand out against blue skies.

Guy Huntington